JUMBLE®
Juggernaut

Classic Puzzles

JUMBLE®

Unscramble these four Jumbles, one letter to
each square, to form four ordinary words.

HILTE

ROARB

NEHBID

GOUTIN

Those outfits cost more than our
whole family clothes budget

WHERE ARE SOME
OF THOSE YUPPIES
RUNNING?

Now arrange the circled letters to form the
surprise answer, as suggested by the above
cartoon.

Print answer here

JUMBLE®

Juggernaut

An Unbeatable Jumble Powerhouse

Henri Arnold,
Bob Lee,
and
Mike Argirion

TRIUMPH
BOOKS

This book is available in quantity at special discounts
for your group or organization.

For further information, contact:

Triumph Books
542 South Dearborn Street
Suite 750
Chicago, Illinois 60605
(312) 939-3330
Fax (312) 663-3557

Printed in U.S.A.

ISBN: 978-1-60078-026-4

Design by Sue Knopf

CONTENTS

JUMBLE®

Unscramble these four Jumbles, one letter to each square, to form four ordinary words.

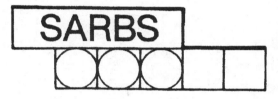

SARBS

CREYM

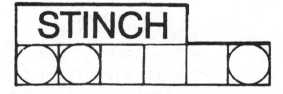

STINCH

LUPHED

IF A MAN MARRIED A WOMAN WITH A TITLE OF NOBILITY, WHAT WOULD HE BE CALLED?

Now arrange the circled letters to form the surprise answer, as suggested by the above cartoon.

Print answer here

JUMBLE

Unscramble these four Jumbles, one letter to each square, to form four ordinary words.

TOHOB

GINOW

HOYNUL

FRIVED

Weren't you supposed to be out jogging today?

APPARENTLY THE EASIEST HABITS TO BREAK ARE THE ONES THAT ARE THIS.

Now arrange the circled letters to form the surprise answer, as suggested by the above cartoon.

Print answer here

JUMBLE®

Unscramble these four Jumbles, one letter to each square, to form four ordinary words.

DYRYL

YUJIC

PUNCKA

ROBUGE

WHAT YOU MIGHT DO WHEN YOU READ A GOOD HORROR STORY.

Now arrange the circled letters to form the surprise answer, as suggested by the above cartoon.

Print answer here "◯◯◯◯◯◯◯" ◯◯ WITH IT

JUMBLE®

Unscramble these four Jumbles, one letter to each square, to form four ordinary words.

OGOIL

TOTID

DEKBEC

INJEYT

ART

INSIDE TRADING

Yeh, dis is where all dem college grads work

RACING

WHAT THE INMATES CALLED THEIR LIBRARY.

Now arrange the circled letters to form the surprise answer, as suggested by the above cartoon.

Print answer here   THE

JUMBLE®

Unscramble these four Jumbles, one letter to
each square, to form four ordinary words.

BAXOR

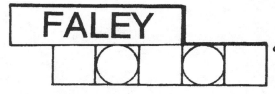

FALEY

NEAFED

DOUSEX

Remember your diet, dear

HE WAS TOLD TO
EAT MORE SEAFOOD,
SO NOW HE EATS
EVERY TIME HE
DOES THIS.

Now arrange the circled letters to form the
surprise answer, as suggested by the above
cartoon.

Print answer here

JUMBLE®

Unscramble these four Jumbles, one letter to
each square, to form four ordinary words.

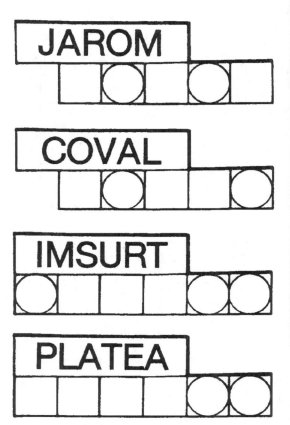

JAROM

COVAL

IMSURT

PLATEA

It's now into the zillions!

THE SUM TOTAL
OF OUR NATIONAL
DEBT IS THIS.

Now arrange the circled letters to form the
surprise answer, as suggested by the above
cartoon.

Print answer here " ◯◯◯◯ ◯◯◯◯◯ ! "

JUMBLE®

Unscramble these four Jumbles, one letter to each square, to form four ordinary words.

TOLCH

USTEA

WENITH

OURSEA

THEY KEPT MINUTES AT THAT MEETING BUT MAN-AGED TO DO THIS.

Now arrange the circled letters to form the surprise answer, as suggested by the above cartoon.

Print answer here

9

JUMBLE®

Unscramble these four Jumbles, one letter to each square, to form four ordinary words.

CANIP

DILEY

WHALLO

LAFTES

PET SHOP

IF YOU DON'T WANT YOUR DOG TO GET RUN OVER, BUY HIM THIS.

Now arrange the circled letters to form the surprise answer, as suggested by the above cartoon.

Print answer here A NEW "  " ON

JUMBLE®

Unscramble these four Jumbles, one letter to
each square, to form four ordinary words.

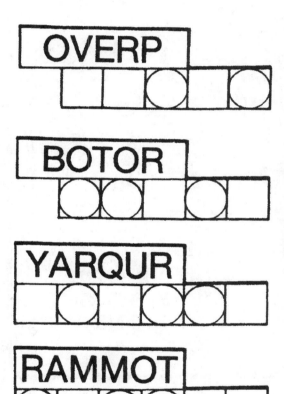

OVERP

BOTOR

YARQUR

RAMMOT

WHAT ALL THAT
GOSSIP AT THE
BOARDING HOUSE
AMOUNTED TO.

Now arrange the circled letters to form the
surprise answer, as suggested by the above
cartoon.

Print answer here

JUMBLE®

Unscramble these four Jumbles, one letter to each square, to form four ordinary words.

GAPAN

MEWNO

SPICET

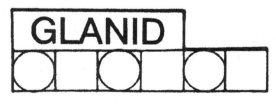

GLANID

Oh, thank you, dear

WHAT HE SAID WHEN HE BOUGHT HER THAT NEW BIKINI.

Now arrange the circled letters to form the surprise answer, as suggested by the above cartoon.

Print answer here IT'S THE  I

JUMBLE®

Unscramble these four Jumbles, one letter to
each square, to form four ordinary words.

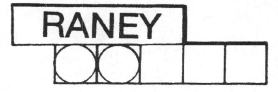
CAROK

RANEY

URQUOM

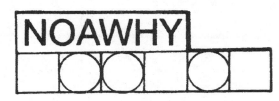
NOAWHY

Please see my secretary
on your way out

WHAT DO DOCTORS
TAKE TO GET RID
OF THE FLU?

Now arrange the circled letters to form the
surprise answer, as suggested by the above
cartoon.

Print answer here

JUMBLE®

Unscramble these four Jumbles, one letter to each square, to form four ordinary words.

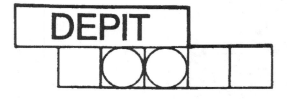

DEPIT

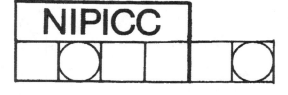

MERFA

NIPICC

WHACES

And another thing...

SHE ROBBED HER HUSBAND OF HIS PEACE OF MIND BY CONSTANTLY GIVING HIM THIS.

Now arrange the circled letters to form the surprise answer, as suggested by the above cartoon.

Print answer here A ⬡⬡⬡⬡⬡ OF ⬡⬡⬡⬡

JUMBLE®

Unscramble these four Jumbles, one letter to
each square, to form four ordinary words.

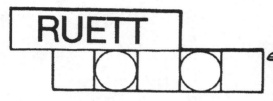
RUETT

FRAWE

SHUHRT

LEFZIZ

AT A BARGAIN
COUNTER, THIS IS
WHAT YOU GET.

Now arrange the circled letters to form the
surprise answer, as suggested by the above
cartoon.

Print answer here  YOU "  "

JUMBLE®

Unscramble these four Jumbles, one letter to
each square, to form four ordinary words.

GOLIC

NIRPT

COULIN

TISMEY

SOME POLITICIANS
COULD HELP THEIR
COUNTRY MORE BY
GETTING THIS.

Now arrange the circled letters to form the
surprise answer, as suggested by the above
cartoon.

Print
answer
here [⬡⬡⬡] OF [⬡⬡⬡⬡⬡⬡⬡⬡]

JUMBLE®

Unscramble these four Jumbles, one letter to each square, to form four ordinary words.

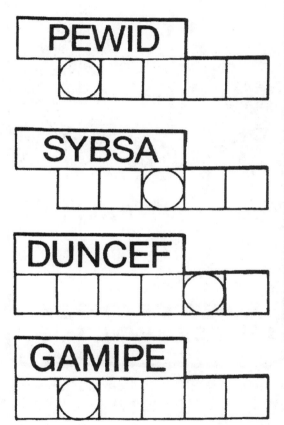

PEWID

SYBSA

DUNCEF

GAMIPE

Hope they get the hint

HOW TO OPEN YOUR MOUTH IN A WAY THAT MIGHT MAKE OTHERS SHUT THEIRS.

Now arrange the circled letters to form the surprise answer, as suggested by the above cartoon.

Print answer here

JUMBLE®

Unscramble these four Jumbles, one letter to
each square, to form four ordinary words.

WEHIN

KNEAT

ANQUIT

SHRUPE

A FEW OF THOSE
CHEESES HAVE THIS.

Now arrange the circled letters to form the
surprise answer, as suggested by the above
cartoon.

Print answer here ⬡⬡⬡⬡⬡ A " ⬡⬡⬡⬡ "

JUMBLE®

Unscramble these four Jumbles, one letter to
each square, to form four ordinary words.

GERAW

HECKO

FALLOR

TYDWAR

WHAT A BIRD DOG
MIGHT BE TRAINED
FOR HUNTING IN.

Now arrange the circled letters to form the
surprise answer, as suggested by the above
cartoon.

Print
answer
here "⬡⬡⬡⬡" ⬡⬡⬡⬡⬡⬡⬡⬡

JUMBLE®

Unscramble these four Jumbles, one letter to
each square, to form four ordinary words.

DROAR

RIHAC

GUBLIN

MUGNIP

THAT STINGY
GOLFER LEFT THE
CADDIE THIS.

MEN'S
LOCKE

Now arrange the circled letters to form the
surprise answer, as suggested by the above
cartoon.

Print answer here ⬡⬡⬡⬡⬡⬡⬡ THE ⬡⬡⬡

JUMBLE®

Unscramble these four Jumbles, one letter to
each square, to form four ordinary words.

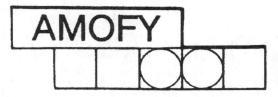

AMOFY

CUVOH

TEABED

YAARTS

We have some nice shellfish tonight

A CRUSTACEAN IS ANOTHER CREATURE THAT MIGHT HAVE THIS.

Now arrange the circled letters to form the
surprise answer, as suggested by the above
cartoon.

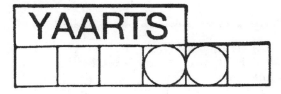

Print answer here A ◯◯◯◯ FOR A ◯◯◯◯

JUMBLE®

Unscramble these four Jumbles, one letter to each square, to form four ordinary words.

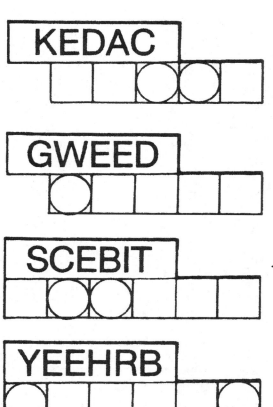

KEDAC

GWEED

SCEBIT

YEEHRB

I kinda liked that little blonde at the party

THIS KEY HAS BEEN KNOWN TO UNLOCK THE TONGUE.

Now arrange the circled letters to form the surprise answer, as suggested by the above cartoon.

Print answer here "◯◯◯◯◯ – ◯◯◯"

JUMBLE®

Unscramble these four Jumbles, one letter to each square, to form four ordinary words.

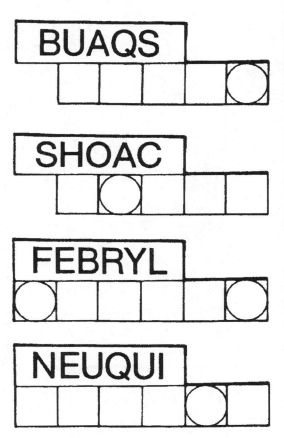

BUAQS

SHOAC

FEBRYL

NEUQUI

ONE WOMAN'S HOBBY MIGHT BE ANOTHER WOMAN'S THIS.

Now arrange the circled letters to form the surprise answer, as suggested by the above cartoon.

Print answer here

JUMBLE®

Unscramble these four Jumbles, one letter to each square, to form four ordinary words.

PEXLE

CUMIS

KELLIY

SOUTID

RUNS ACROSS THE FLOOR ALTHOUGH IT CAN'T WALK.

Now arrange the circled letters to form the surprise answer, as suggested by the above cartoon.

Print answer here

JUMBLE®

Unscramble these four Jumbles, one letter to each square, to form four ordinary words.

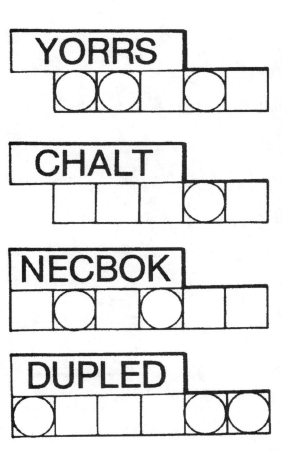

YORRS

CHALT

NECBOK

DUPLED

WHAT DAVID DECIDED TO DO WHEN GOLIATH STARTED LOOKING TIRED.

Now arrange the circled letters to form the surprise answer, as suggested by the above cartoon.

Print answer here "⬡⬡⬡⬡" HIM TO ⬡⬡⬡⬡⬡⬡

JUMBLE®

Unscramble these four Jumbles, one letter to each square, to form four ordinary words.

RANOB

CINEE

SLAVNY

POOSUR

WHAT KIND OF MARKS DID YOU GET IN PHYSICAL EDUCATION?

Now arrange the circled letters to form the surprise answer, as suggested by the above cartoon.

Print answer here " ⃝⃝⃝⃝ A FEW ⃝⃝⃝⃝⃝⃝⃝⃝ "

JUMBLE®

Juggernaut

Daily Puzzles

JUMBLE®

Unscramble these four Jumbles, one letter to each square, to form four ordinary words.

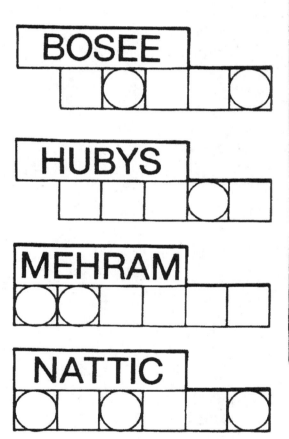

BOSEE

HUBYS

MEHRAM

NATTIC

IF HORSEBACK RIDING BECOMES AN "ADDICTION," THIS CAN BE EXPENSIVE.

Now arrange the circled letters to form the surprise answer, as suggested by the above cartoon.

Print answer here

JUMBLE®

Unscramble these four Jumbles, one letter to each square, to form four ordinary words.

LIWLT

DIGUL

GONBEE

ROOHRR

It won't be long now

THE GROOM WAS FIT TO BE TIED...

Now arrange the circled letters to form the surprise answer, as suggested by the above cartoon.

Print answer here

JUMBLE®

Unscramble these four Jumbles, one letter to each square, to form four ordinary words.

UGSIE

DONUP

HINGKT

PEMEXT

They have a lot to learn

THEIR INVOLVEMENT WITH DIVING WAS ONLY THIS.

Now arrange the circled letters to form the surprise answer, as suggested by the above cartoon.

Print answer here

JUMBLE®

Unscramble these four Jumbles, one letter to each square, to form four ordinary words.

ORPOD

GURPE

LAMORN

RAUFIN

NOW IN ITS TENTH YEAR!

A THEATER OWNER NEVER SUFFERS IN THIS.

Now arrange the circled letters to form the surprise answer, as suggested by the above cartoon.

Print answer here THE " ☐☐☐☐ ☐☐☐ "

JUMBLE®

Unscramble these four Jumbles, one letter to each square, to form four ordinary words.

SEECA

TILMI

PANTIC

NORRAC

(Sniff) There goes the atmosphere again!

WHAT THOSE OLD-FASHIONED STOCK-YARDS USED TO HAVE ABOUT THEM.

Now arrange the circled letters to form the surprise answer, as suggested by the above cartoon.

Print answer here A ⬡⬡⬡⬡⬡⬡⬡ " ⬡⬡⬡ "

JUMBLE®

Unscramble these four Jumbles, one letter to
each square, to form four ordinary words.

YURLT

WOSON

BAHFLE

DANNIL

WHAT MANY DRY
SPEECHES ARE.

Now arrange the circled letters to form the
surprise answer, as suggested by the above
cartoon.

Print answer here ◯◯◯ ◯◯◯

JUMBLE®

Unscramble these four Jumbles, one letter to each square, to form four ordinary words.

YUINF

KWATE

THROOC

SNIDUM

Out of the way, you little pip-squeak

THINK BEFORE YOU SPEAK. THEN...

Now arrange the circled letters to form the surprise answer, as suggested by the above cartoon.

Print answer here

34

JUMBLE®

Unscramble these four Jumbles, one letter to each square, to form four ordinary words.

ADEHA

BRUTS

TEPPIC

NAHDDE

It's back to the straight and narrow for you

THE DOCTOR SAID THE PATIENT'S HEART WAS THIS.

Now arrange the circled letters to form the surprise answer, as suggested by the above cartoon.

Print answer here OFF THE " ◯◯◯◯◯◯◯ " ◯◯◯◯

JUMBLE.

Unscramble these four Jumbles, one letter to each square, to form four ordinary words.

MAGDO

YARDT

HINGAC

TEPLES

A diet would be better

THE BEST
WEIGHT LIFTERS.

Now arrange the circled letters to form the surprise answer, as suggested by the above cartoon.

Print answer here

JUMBLE®

Unscramble these four Jumbles, one letter to each square, to form four ordinary words.

ULIPP

INBAC

STEGAK

CUBEKT

Yes, dear—we've already gone over that

CLICK!

WHEN ALL IS SAID AND DONE, SOME PEOPLE JUST DO THIS.

Now arrange the circled letters to form the surprise answer, as suggested by the above cartoon.

Print answer here

◯◯◯◯ ON ◯◯◯◯◯◯◯◯

JUMBLE®

Unscramble these four Jumbles, one letter to each square, to form four ordinary words.

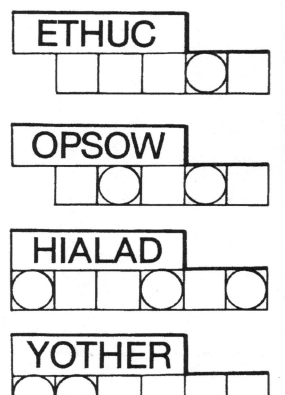

ETHUC

OPSOW

HIALAD

YOTHER

Everything is working out fine

HE'S THE "MASTER" IN HIS OWN HOME JUST SO LONG AS HE DOES THIS.

Now arrange the circled letters to form the surprise answer, as suggested by the above cartoon.

Print answer here ⬡⬡⬡⬡ HE'S ⬡⬡⬡⬡

JUMBLE®

Unscramble these four Jumbles, one letter to
each square, to form four ordinary words.

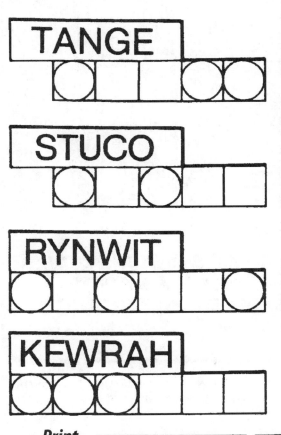

TANGE

STUCO

RYNWIT

KEWRAH

MONEY CAN BE
LOST IN MORE THIS.

Now arrange the circled letters to form the
surprise answer, as suggested by the above
cartoon.

**Print
answer
here**
⬚⬚⬚⬚ ⬚⬚⬚⬚ " ⬚⬚⬚ "

JUMBLE.

Unscramble these four Jumbles, one letter to each square, to form four ordinary words.

ALIVA

IRATT

GABLEN

MODCEY

THEY SAID THE MOVIE HAD A HAPPY ENDING BECAUSE EVERYONE WAS THIS.

Now arrange the circled letters to form the surprise answer, as suggested by the above cartoon.

Print answer here ◯◯◯◯◯ IT WAS ◯◯◯◯◯

JUMBLE®

Unscramble these four Jumbles, one letter to
each square, to form four ordinary words.

RINED
⬜⬜⬜⬜⬜

AMDAM
⬜⬜⬜⬜⬜

GELIGG
⬜⬜⬜⬜⬜⬜

HAPNOR
⬜⬜⬜⬜⬜⬜

WHAT THAT ECCENTRIC
DOOR-TO-DOOR
SALESMAN MUST
HAVE BEEN.

Now arrange the circled letters to form the
surprise answer, as suggested by the above
cartoon.

Print
answer
here ⬜ " ⬜⬜⬜⬜ – ⬜⬜⬜⬜ "

JUMBLE®

Unscramble these four Jumbles, one letter to each square, to form four ordinary words.

REVUC

TAWLZ

SCULIE

BUTSOE

HE DINES WITH
THE UPPER SET
AND IS APT TO
DO THIS, TOO.

Now arrange the circled letters to form the surprise answer, as suggested by the above cartoon.

Print answer here ◯◯◯ HIS ◯◯◯◯◯◯

JUMBLE®

Unscramble these four Jumbles, one letter to each square, to form four ordinary words.

INGAR

TUMOH

LOUBED

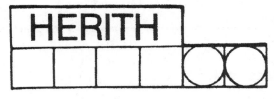

HERITH

WHAT THE GUY WHO WAS HER "IDEAL" BECAME AFTER THEY GOT MARRIED.

Now arrange the circled letters to form the surprise answer, as suggested by the above cartoon.

Print answer here

43

JUMBLE®

Unscramble these four Jumbles, one letter to
each square, to form four ordinary words.

VOLEH

DUGIE

AFAIRS

TELRUT

WHY HE TOOK
THE SCREENS OFF
HIS WINDOWS.

Now arrange the circled letters to form the
surprise answer, as suggested by the above
cartoon.

*Print
answer
here*

TO ⬡⬡⬡ THE ⬡⬡⬡⬡⬡⬡ ⬡⬡⬡

JUMBLE®

Unscramble these four Jumbles, one letter to each square, to form four ordinary words.

UPYPP

VEFER

GALEEB

SENNIG

Guess I'll turn in

THE ONLY TIME THAT CROOK'S ON THE LEVEL IS WHEN HE'S THIS.

Now arrange the circled letters to form the surprise answer, as suggested by the above cartoon.

Print answer here

JUMBLE®

Unscramble these four Jumbles, one letter to each square, to form four ordinary words.

GREBA

RAUZE

DEBBAL

LEWLOY

Ten years! Next case!

HE WANTED TO BECOME A LAWYER BADLY, BUT HE ENDED UP BECOMING THIS.

Now arrange the circled letters to form the surprise answer, as suggested by the above cartoon.

Print answer here A ⟨◯◯◯ ◯◯◯◯◯◯⟩

JUMBLE®

Unscramble these four Jumbles, one letter to each square, to form four ordinary words.

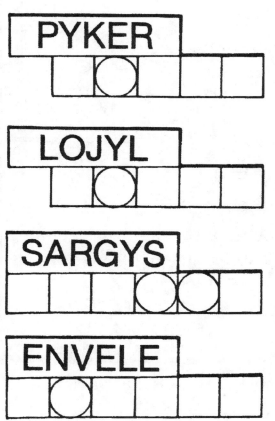

PYKER

LOJYL

SARGYS

ENVELE

(Sob) I'll never speak to him again!

ANY MAN WHO ARGUES WITH HIS WIFE AND WINS...

Now arrange the circled letters to form the surprise answer, as suggested by the above cartoon.

Print answer here

JUMBLE®

Unscramble these four Jumbles, one letter to
each square, to form four ordinary words.

RIVOY

THIGE

VIEWEL

DAMNET

Guess I made an idiot
of myself last night

WHEN YOU "LIVE IT
UP," YOU MIGHT
TRY TO DO THIS
AFTERWARD.

Now arrange the circled letters to form the
surprise answer, as suggested by the above
cartoon.

Print answer here ⟨◯◯◯◯◯⟩ ⟨◯◯⟩ ⟨◯◯◯◯◯⟩

JUMBLE®

Unscramble these four Jumbles, one letter to each square, to form four ordinary words.

OSPOT

EBBIR

GRANDO

TRUXAS

DIPPING YOUR BREAD INTO GRAVY MAY BE BAD MANNERS, BUT IT'S CERTAINLY ALSO THIS.

Now arrange the circled letters to form the surprise answer, as suggested by the above cartoon.

Print answer here " ⬡⬡⬡⬡ ⬡⬡⬡⬡⬡ "

JUMBLE®

Unscramble these four Jumbles, one letter to each square, to form four ordinary words.

YARAR

LAVEG

MYDOBE

RUVESS

A MAN WHO CLAIMS HE NEVER MAKES A MISTAKE ISN'T THIS.

Now arrange the circled letters to form the surprise answer, as suggested by the above cartoon.

Print answer here

JUMBLE®

Unscramble these four Jumbles, one letter to
each square, to form four ordinary words.

MEPOT

EATAB

TRAUGI

LESPEN

Doesn't
look
like
much !

A BIKINI NEVER
ATTRACTS ATTENTION
UNTIL SOMEONE
DOES THIS.

Now arrange the circled letters to form the
surprise answer, as suggested by the above
cartoon.

Print answer here

51

JUMBLE®

Unscramble these four Jumbles, one letter to
each square, to form four ordinary words.

SOGEO

USAME

YARVOS

HUBLES

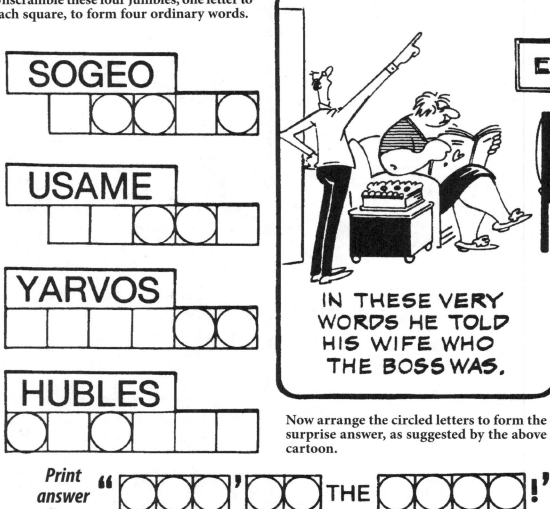

IN THESE VERY
WORDS HE TOLD
HIS WIFE WHO
THE BOSS WAS.

Now arrange the circled letters to form the
surprise answer, as suggested by the above
cartoon.

Print
answer
here "◯◯◯'◯◯THE◯◯◯◯!"

JUMBLE®

Unscramble these four Jumbles, one letter to each square, to form four ordinary words.

TAUID

CERDY

MYNITE

ROBRAW

THAT LONELY GUY
ROBBED A BANK
JUST SO HE COULD
FEEL THIS.

Now arrange the circled letters to form the surprise answer, as suggested by the above cartoon.

Print answer here " ◯◯◯◯◯◯ "

JUMBLE®

Unscramble these four Jumbles, one letter to
each square, to form four ordinary words.

BOMUG

RARBI

KRODEF

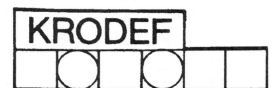

THORCC

KWIKKY DINNERS

SHE CAN DISH IT
OUT, BUT CAN SHE
DO THIS?

Now arrange the circled letters to form the
surprise answer, as suggested by the above
cartoon.

Print answer here

54

JUMBLE®

Unscramble these four Jumbles, one letter to each square, to form four ordinary words.

GEMID

URUGA

SCUSID

TENGLE

Here's your new regimen

WHEN THEY REACH MIDDLE AGE, MANY PEOPLE ARE REDUCED TO THIS.

Now arrange the circled letters to form the surprise answer, as suggested by the above cartoon.

Print answer here

JUMBLE®

Unscramble these four Jumbles, one letter to each square, to form four ordinary words.

HOACC

LEKAN

RITAUN

VODURE

She looks lovely, but...

Shhh!

THE BEST WAY TO TELL A WOMAN'S AGE IS WHEN SHE'S THIS.

Now arrange the circled letters to form the surprise answer, as suggested by the above cartoon.

Print answer here

JUMBLE®

Unscramble these four Jumbles, one letter to each square, to form four ordinary words.

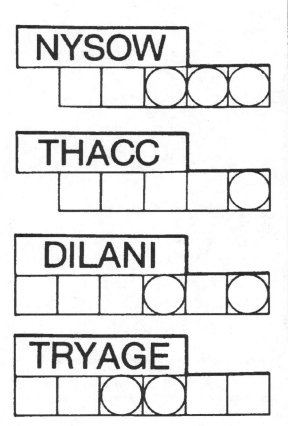

NYSOW

THACC

DILANI

TRYAGE

Here's a dime—go out and mow my lawn

HOW THE MISER GOT RICH.

Now arrange the circled letters to form the surprise answer, as suggested by the above cartoon.

 *Print answer here* THE " ⬡⬡⬡⬡⬡ " ⬡⬡⬡

JUMBLE®

Unscramble these four Jumbles, one letter to each square, to form four ordinary words.

NIHKT

INVEX

SMEFLY

FAISAR

These new forms are something else

WHAT THE FISHERMAN'S GROSS INCOME WAS.

Now arrange the circled letters to form the surprise answer, as suggested by the above cartoon.

Print answer here

 AS  "  "

JUMBLE®

Unscramble these four Jumbles, one letter to each square, to form four ordinary words.

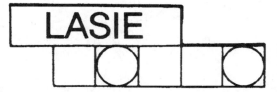

LASIE

CHACO

GERROF

SUREDS

There'll be others who will have the real power

WHAT THAT MATH WHIZ WHO ROSE TO THE TOP OF THE FIRM ENDED UP AS.

Now arrange the circled letters to form the surprise answer, as suggested by the above cartoon.

Print answer here THE ⬡⬡⬡⬡⬡⬡⬡⬡⬡⬡⬡

JUMBLE®

Unscramble these four Jumbles, one letter to each square, to form four ordinary words.

DYNAH

MAUSE

WOELLY

SUDSIC

SLAP!

Hey!

WHAT THE HIGHWAY MAINTENANCE MAN WAS TOLD TO DO.

Now arrange the circled letters to form the surprise answer, as suggested by the above cartoon.

Print answer here

"   "

JUMBLE®

Unscramble these four Jumbles, one letter to
each square, to form four ordinary words.

KAFLE

LOMOB

TRUFUE

ENGOUT

HOW TO SILENCE
A "LOUD" TIE.

Now arrange the circled letters to form the
surprise answer, as suggested by the above
cartoon.

*Print
answer
here* ◯◯◯ A " ◯◯◯◯◯◯◯ "

JUMBLE®

Unscramble these four Jumbles, one letter to each square, to form four ordinary words.

RYRUH

NOIBS

STRAIG

DROFEK

A risky way to make a living, I'd say

WHAT THE PRO-FESSIONAL CRAP-SHOOTER'S BUSINESS MUST HAVE BEEN.

Now arrange the circled letters to form the surprise answer, as suggested by the above cartoon.

Print answer here " ◯◯◯◯◯ "

JUMBLE®

Unscramble these four Jumbles, one letter to each square, to form four ordinary words.

WETHA

LAIDY

GUYSAR

NIRGIF

THE HORSE YOU
PUT YOUR MONEY
ON OFTEN
DOES THIS.

Now arrange the circled letters to form the surprise answer, as suggested by the above cartoon.

Print answer here

WITH

63

JUMBLE®

Unscramble these four Jumbles, one letter to each square, to form four ordinary words.

HAABS

THANC

YAMSIL

LOFUND

A STUBBORN MAN DOESN'T HOLD OPINIONS...

Now arrange the circled letters to form the surprise answer, as suggested by the above cartoon.

Print answer here THEY

JUMBLE®

Unscramble these four Jumbles, one letter to
each square, to form four ordinary words.

ZIMEA

LAVIE

VARQUE

FATSIE

Good old Cousin Elmer sure struck it big

IN ADDITION TO MONEY, THE RICH NEVER SEEM TO LACK THIS.

Now arrange the circled letters to form the
surprise answer, as suggested by the above
cartoon.

Print answer here

65

JUMBLE®

Unscramble these four Jumbles, one letter to
each square, to form four ordinary words.

NYLOP

WETET

AHLEEX

SEDGIT

WHAT THE SENTRY
AT THE ARMY
KITCHEN KEPT.

Now arrange the circled letters to form the
surprise answer, as suggested by the above
cartoon.

*Print
answer
here*   HIS ☐☐☐☐ " ☐☐☐☐☐☐☐ "

JUMBLE®

Unscramble these four Jumbles, one letter to
each square, to form four ordinary words.

MARAD

INSAB

GOOSTE

YASUNE

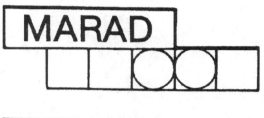

It's a long wait, but worth it

IS SHE A GOOD
DRESSMAKER?

Now arrange the circled letters to form the
surprise answer, as suggested by the above
cartoon.

Print answer here  " "

JUMBLE®

Unscramble these four Jumbles, one letter to each square, to form four ordinary words.

DEYNE

CUNDE

LIFFUT

EMORCH

HE WAS A FRIEND OF THE OWNER, WHICH IS WHY HE GOT EVERYTHING...

Now arrange the circled letters to form the surprise answer, as suggested by the above cartoon.

Print answer here ☐☐ ☐☐☐ " ☐☐☐☐ "

JUMBLE®

Unscramble these four Jumbles, one letter to each square, to form four ordinary words.

CAMPH

TUILB

LIKLER

ERTOPY

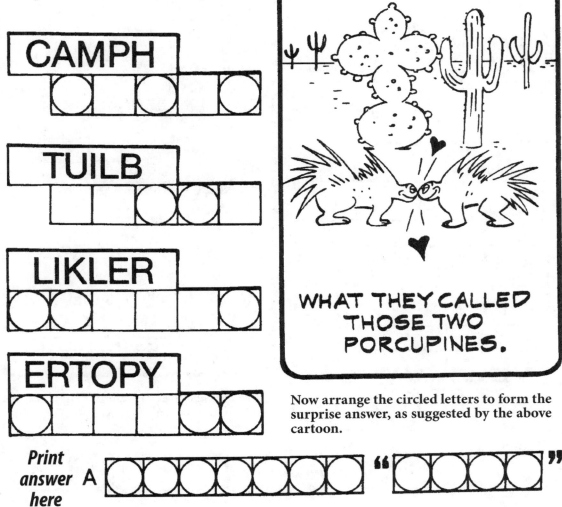

WHAT THEY CALLED THOSE TWO PORCUPINES.

Now arrange the circled letters to form the surprise answer, as suggested by the above cartoon.

Print answer here A ⬡⬡⬡⬡⬡⬡⬡ "⬡⬡⬡⬡"

JUMBLE®

Unscramble these four Jumbles, one letter to
each square, to form four ordinary words.

MENGO

JUTSO

KAUMPE

VEGASA

STICKS TO ONE
THING AND HOPE-
FULLY GETS THERE.

Now arrange the circled letters to form the
surprise answer, as suggested by the above
cartoon.

Print answer here

JUMBLE®

Unscramble these four Jumbles, one letter to each square, to form four ordinary words.

OUMID

NAJOB

CURSIC

PANPHE

Take 'er up

WHAT TO TIE UP THAT GRAND WITH.

Now arrange the circled letters to form the surprise answer, as suggested by the above cartoon.

Print answer here

 "  "

JUMBLE®

Unscramble these four Jumbles, one letter to
each square, to form four ordinary words.

GINOR

ENYAH

NITTEK

TORREC

Maybe now they'll
behave themselves

THEY'VE IMPROVED
THE TRAINS TO
WASHINGTON SO THAT
THE POLITICIANS
CAN NOW DO THIS.

Now arrange the circled letters to form the
surprise answer, as suggested by the above
cartoon.

*Print
answer
here*
GET
ON THE

JUMBLE®

Unscramble these four Jumbles, one letter to
each square, to form four ordinary words.

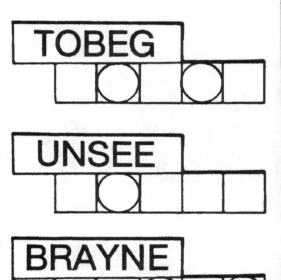

TOBEG

UNSEE

BRAYNE

DIRAUM

SHE USED TO BE
AFRAID OF MICE
UNTIL SHE FINALLY
DECIDED TO DO THIS.

Now arrange the circled letters to form the
surprise answer, as suggested by the above
cartoon.

Print answer here

73

JUMBLE®

Unscramble these four Jumbles, one letter to each square, to form four ordinary words.

WILEH

TRAFE

BYSUIL

HUMBAS

WHAT'S THAT UNDER-GROUND MOVEMENT THAT'S GOING ON IN MANY CITIES?

Now arrange the circled letters to form the surprise answer, as suggested by the above cartoon.

Print answer here ◯◯◯ ◯◯◯◯◯◯

JUMBLE®

Unscramble these four Jumbles, one letter to each square, to form four ordinary words.

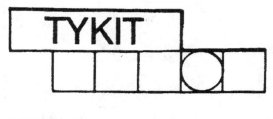

TYKIT

BYGAG

NIPURT

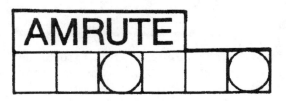

AMRUTE

WALL ST.

ONE SURE WAY
TO BEAT THE
STOCK MARKET.

Now arrange the circled letters to form the surprise answer, as suggested by the above cartoon.

Print answer here JUST "  ! "

JUMBLE®

Unscramble these four Jumbles, one letter to each square, to form four ordinary words.

LAVEE

AUPSE

TERRFE

WARROH

WHAT A RAINY DAY IS FOR A CAB DRIVER.

Now arrange the circled letters to form the surprise answer, as suggested by the above cartoon.

Print answer here " ☐☐☐☐ " ☐☐☐☐☐☐☐☐

JUMBLE®

Unscramble these four Jumbles, one letter to each square, to form four ordinary words.

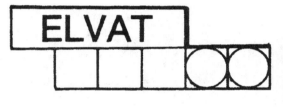

ELVAT

RUHYR

PAWDUR

BISMUT

THE PESSIMIST WAS HANGING AROUND THE DELICATESSEN STORE BECAUSE HE WAS WAITING FOR THIS.

Now arrange the circled letters to form the surprise answer, as suggested by the above cartoon.

Print answer here  " "

JUMBLE®

Unscramble these four Jumbles, one letter to each square, to form four ordinary words.

FEBIT

UPYTT

VENAHE

LOWLAF

WHAT A GOOD
POLICE DOG
MIGHT PUT.

Now arrange the circled letters to form the surprise answer, as suggested by the above cartoon.

Print answer here ◯◯◯◯◯ INTO THE ◯◯◯

JUMBLE®

Unscramble these four Jumbles, one letter to each square, to form four ordinary words.

SUDOE

DOLOB

YALWEE

TRIAFY

Er... uh...

EVERY TIME HE HAS AN ARGUMENT WITH HIS WIFE, THIS HAPPENS.

Now arrange the circled letters to form the surprise answer, as suggested by the above cartoon.

Print answer here

☐☐☐☐☐ "☐☐☐☐☐" HIM

JUMBLE®

Unscramble these four Jumbles, one letter to each square, to form four ordinary words.

OSKET

ADDIE

NESSUC

CLOASE

WHAT THE SHIP'S DOCTORS GENERALLY DO.

Now arrange the circled letters to form the surprise answer, as suggested by the above cartoon.

Print answer here " ◯◯◯ ◯◯◯◯◯◯◯◯ "

JUMBLE®

Unscramble these four Jumbles, one letter to
each square, to form four ordinary words.

YOFAR

SHLYP

DULANO

NYLARX

IF YOU BECOME
ADDICTED TO
WRESTLING, IT
MIGHT DO THIS.

Now arrange the circled letters to form the
surprise answer, as suggested by the above
cartoon.

Print answer here GET
A ☐☐☐☐ ON ☐☐☐

JUMBLE®

Unscramble these four Jumbles, one letter to
each square, to form four ordinary words.

FIRGE

□□◯◯□

SUHOE

□◯□□□

ORTETT

◯□◯◯□□

CUNNEA

◯□◯◯□□

HE MARRIED A
RICH WIFE, SO HE
NEVER HAD TO PAY
ANYTHING — EXCEPT
THIS.

Now arrange the circled letters to form the
surprise answer, as suggested by the above
cartoon.

Print answer here   ◯◯◯◯◯◯◯◯◯◯

JUMBLE®

Unscramble these four Jumbles, one letter to each square, to form four ordinary words.

VARGE

DOPKE

RUBETT

CLAISO

WHAT THE CANINE
MEMBER OF THE
BOY SCOUTS
WAS CALLED.

Now arrange the circled letters to form the surprise answer, as suggested by the above cartoon.

Print answer here A " ◯◯◯◯◯ " ◯◯◯◯◯

JUMBLE®

Unscramble these four Jumbles, one letter to
each square, to form four ordinary words.

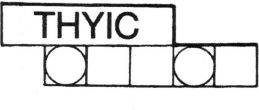

THYIC

CEHKT

GUIFER

KLEACT

HE THOUGHT HE
WAS A WIT, AND
MOST OF THEM
SAID HE WAS THIS.

Now arrange the circled letters to form the
surprise answer, as suggested by the above
cartoon.

Print answer here

JUMBLE®

Unscramble these four Jumbles, one letter to each square, to form four ordinary words.

KLANB

TWAHR

YACENG

JOLTES

DEPARTURES

ZABAUTIA JIMTUCTOO

WHAT THE ROBBER TRIED TO DO AFTER HE STOLE ALL THE MONEY.

Now arrange the circled letters to form the surprise answer, as suggested by the above cartoon.

Print answer here "⃝⃝⃝⃝⃝" ⃝⃝⃝⃝

JUMBLE®

Unscramble these four Jumbles, one letter to
each square, to form four ordinary words.

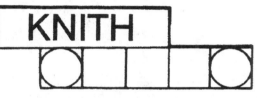

KNITH

PEROW

SURJIT

VURSCY

DOES YOUR WIFE
PICK YOUR CLOTHES?

Acme Tailors

Now arrange the circled letters to form the
surprise answer, as suggested by the above
cartoon.

Print
answer
here

" ⬡⬡⬡⬡ THE ⬡⬡⬡⬡⬡⬡⬡⬡ "

JUMBLE®

Unscramble these four Jumbles, one letter to
each square, to form four ordinary words.

VERIP

SOINY

NEPPIS

ENCHIL

HE TRIED TO KISS
HER, BUT SHE'D
HAVE THIS.

Now arrange the circled letters to form the
surprise answer, as suggested by the above
cartoon.

Print answer here ☐☐☐☐ OF ☐☐☐ ☐☐☐

JUMBLE®

Unscramble these four Jumbles, one letter to each square, to form four ordinary words.

BISCA

TILUQ

DYOMLE

CAPTER

WHAT LACE
SHOULD NEVER BE.

Now arrange the circled letters to form the surprise answer, as suggested by the above cartoon.

Print answer here ⬡⬡⬡ OF "⬡-⬡⬡⬡⬡"

JUMBLE®

Unscramble these four Jumbles, one letter to
each square, to form four ordinary words.

GIRRO

WYSEN

SNUIGE

YIRRAT

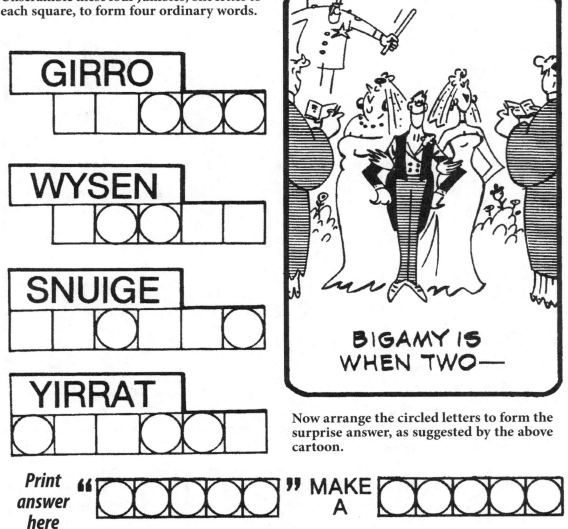

BIGAMY IS
WHEN TWO—

Now arrange the circled letters to form the
surprise answer, as suggested by the above
cartoon.

Print
answer
here " ☐☐☐☐☐ " MAKE
A ☐☐☐☐☐

JUMBLE®

Unscramble these four Jumbles, one letter to each square, to form four ordinary words.

MONDE

YURST

SWERKE

FISHET

WHEN YOU TRY TO
WASH A SMALL
KID, HE'S APT TO
DO THIS.

Now arrange the circled letters to form the surprise answer, as suggested by the above cartoon.

Print answer here  IT

JUMBLE®

Unscramble these four Jumbles, one letter to each square, to form four ordinary words.

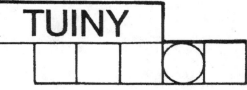
TUINY

ROUCS

KNABIG

PARMEC

SOME AGING
THESPIANS MIGHT
FIND IT DIFFICULT
TO DO THIS.

Now arrange the circled letters to form the surprise answer, as suggested by the above cartoon.

Print answer here  ◯◯◯ THEIR ◯◯◯

JUMBLE®

Unscramble these four Jumbles, one letter to
each square, to form four ordinary words.

PUTER

LOHLE

NUSIAD

LEYRAR

It took brains to
get where he is

ONE WAY TO GET
AHEAD AND STAY
AHEAD IS TO
DO THIS.

Now arrange the circled letters to form the
surprise answer, as suggested by the above
cartoon.

Print answer here

92

JUMBLE®

Unscramble these four Jumbles, one letter to
each square, to form four ordinary words.

GUBOS

HASUQ

TESKUM

WHAT LEGAL
"TENDER" MIGHT
BE WHEN YOU
DON'T HAVE IT.

GLERCY

Now arrange the circled letters to form the
surprise answer, as suggested by the above
cartoon.

Print answer here "  "

JUMBLE®

Unscramble these four Jumbles, one letter to
each square, to form four ordinary words.

KUSHY

LAGIE

TAUBEY

BIMEBI

IN THOSE DAYS A
WOMAN WOULD RAISE
A HEM IN ORDER
TO DO THIS.

Now arrange the circled letters to form the
surprise answer, as suggested by the above
cartoon.

Print answer here ☐☐☐☐ ☐ " ☐☐☐ "

JUMBLE®

Unscramble these four Jumbles, one letter to each square, to form four ordinary words.

ARATO

GOARC

REDOWP

INROUJ

ANOTHER NAME FOR A CLOUDBURST.

Now arrange the circled letters to form the surprise answer, as suggested by the above cartoon.

Print answer here A " ⬭⬭⬭⬭⬭ ⬭⬭⬭⬭ "

JUMBLE®

Unscramble these four Jumbles, one letter to each square, to form four ordinary words.

BUJOM

CITOX

SHORCC

PACRIY

Tee hee

SOMETHING OFTEN FOUND IN NEWS-PAPERS AND ON BEACHES.

Now arrange the circled letters to form the surprise answer, as suggested by the above cartoon.

Print answer here

A ☐☐☐☐☐ " ☐☐☐☐☐☐ "

JUMBLE®

Unscramble these four Jumbles, one letter to
each square, to form four ordinary words.

LAFAT

YIZZD

FROMIN

TIPIDE

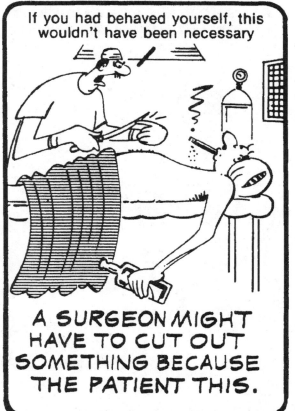

If you had behaved yourself, this
wouldn't have been necessary

A SURGEON MIGHT
HAVE TO CUT OUT
SOMETHING BECAUSE
THE PATIENT THIS.

Now arrange the circled letters to form the
surprise answer, as suggested by the above
cartoon.

Print answer here

JUMBLE®

Unscramble these four Jumbles, one letter to
each square, to form four ordinary words.

ALYMN

GLIEB

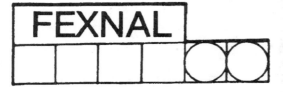

FEXNAL

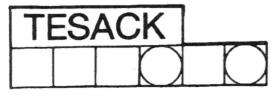

TESACK

MOST PEOPLE ARE
PUT OUT WHEN
THEY'RE THIS.

Now arrange the circled letters to form the
surprise answer, as suggested by the above
cartoon.

Print answer here

JUMBLE

Unscramble these four Jumbles, one letter to
each square, to form four ordinary words.

MOVEN

SEMYS

DREHWS

LOUTTE

WHAT DO YOU GET
WHEN A MONSTER
STEPS ON A HOUSE?

Now arrange the circled letters to form the
surprise answer, as suggested by the above
cartoon.

*Print
answer
here* " ◯◯◯◯◯◯ ◯◯◯◯◯ "

JUMBLE®

Unscramble these four Jumbles, one letter to each square, to form four ordinary words.

LEWJE

PLIMB

GINRAD

UNPOCE

Remember, that's supposed to be a binding agreement

JUSTICE PEACE

WHAT A MARRIAGE CERTIFICATE SHOULD BE WRITTEN ON.

Now arrange the circled letters to form the surprise answer, as suggested by the above cartoon.

Print answer here "  "

JUMBLE®

Unscramble these four Jumbles, one letter to
each square, to form four ordinary words.

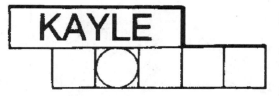

KAYLE

LURBY

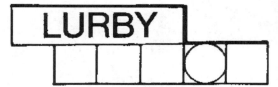

YEUFLE

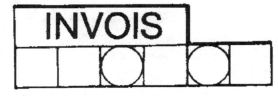

INVOIS

Freshly
caught

WHAT WERE THE
SHOEMAKER'S TWO
FAVORITE KINDS
OF FISH?

Now arrange the circled letters to form the
surprise answer, as suggested by the above
cartoon.

Print answer here

JUMBLE®

Unscramble these four Jumbles, one letter to each square, to form four ordinary words.

LULBY

IGNAT

OSANTA

MEEDUR

You'll love me when I'm old and gray?

HE PROMISED FIRST THAT HE WOULD BE THIS.

Now arrange the circled letters to form the surprise answer, as suggested by the above cartoon.

Print answer here ⟨◯◯◯◯⟩ TO THE ⟨◯◯◯◯⟩

JUMBLE®

Unscramble these four Jumbles, one letter to
each square, to form four ordinary words.

EGBIE

TASHY

CUSTOC

RELOAP

A PEA-SOUPY FOG
MAY GIVE
MOTORISTS THIS.

Now arrange the circled letters to form the
surprise answer, as suggested by the above
cartoon.

Print answer here ⬡⬡⬡ " ⬡⬡⬡⬡⬡⬡⬡ "

JUMBLE®

Unscramble these four Jumbles, one letter to each square, to form four ordinary words.

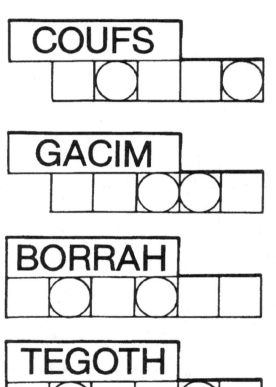

COUFS

GACIM

BORRAH

TEGOTH

You don't have to come back after lunch

He's been paying him half a million a year

MIGHT ALSO BE "FIRED"...EVEN WHEN SEEMINGLY THIS.

Now arrange the circled letters to form the surprise answer, as suggested by the above cartoon.

Print answer here ◯ "◯◯◯◯"

JUMBLE

Unscramble these four Jumbles, one letter to
each square, to form four ordinary words.

YOAPS

VAMUE

THYFOR

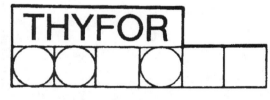

PERTIL

I don't approve!

You're just jealous

THE YOUNGER
GENERATION ALWAYS
SEEMS MORE OUT-
RAGEOUS WHEN ONE
IS NO LONGER THIS.

Now arrange the circled letters to form the
surprise answer, as suggested by the above
cartoon.

Print answer here

105

JUMBLE®

Unscramble these four Jumbles, one letter to
each square, to form four ordinary words.

FLOTY

CIKHT

TASSID

LAPRIL

WHAT HE GOT AS A
RESULT OF
CARELESS DRIVING.

Now arrange the circled letters to form the
surprise answer, as suggested by the above
cartoon.

Print answer here ◯ " ◯◯◯ ◯◯◯◯ "

JUMBLE®

Unscramble these four Jumbles, one letter to each square, to form four ordinary words.

RUFOL

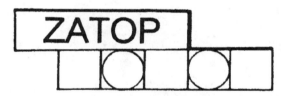

ZATOP

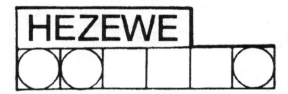

HEZEWE

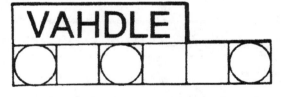

VAHDLE

I got it!

There he goes again!

THAT WISEACRE HAS THE SOLUTION TO EVERY DIFFICULT PROBLEM RIGHT IN THIS.

Now arrange the circled letters to form the surprise answer, as suggested by the above cartoon.

Print answer here THE ⬡⬡⬡⬡⬡⬡ OF HIS ⬡⬡⬡⬡

JUMBLE®

Unscramble these four Jumbles, one letter to
each square, to form four ordinary words.

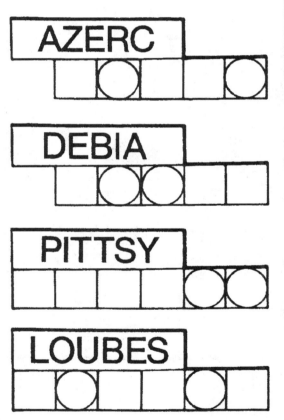

AZERC

DEBIA

PITTSY

LOUBES

WHAT IGNORANCE
AT THE BEACH IS.

Now arrange the circled letters to form the
surprise answer, as suggested by the above
cartoon.

Print answer here " ☐☐☐☐☐☐ – ☐☐☐ "

JUMBLE®

Unscramble these four Jumbles, one letter to
each square, to form four ordinary words.

DROAH

KRIPE

TEOGUN

HALINE

She has a good record

WHY THE
BURLESQUE QUEEN
DECIDED TO RUN
FOR OFFICE.

Now arrange the circled letters to form the
surprise answer, as suggested by the above
cartoon.

Print
answer
here

SHE
HAD

TO

JUMBLE®

Unscramble these four Jumbles, one letter to
each square, to form four ordinary words.

YOILD

ORRUJ

INVOIL

CHYSIP

No, thanks—I'm
on the wagon

JAXCO.
ANNUAL PICNIC

WHAT HAPPENS
EVERY TIME HE
TURNS OVER A
NEW LEAF?

Now arrange the circled letters to form the
surprise answer, as suggested by the above
cartoon.

Print answer here IT'S

JUMBLE®

Unscramble these four Jumbles, one letter to
each square, to form four ordinary words.

VERBA

NOOLC

EUGLED

DAGOIA

THIS MIGHT HELP
A GAMBLER WIN
A GOOD DEAL
OF CHIPS.

Now arrange the circled letters to form the
surprise answer, as suggested by the above
cartoon.

Print answer here

JUMBLE®

Unscramble these four Jumbles, one letter to each square, to form four ordinary words.

VENOL

SINUM

TOWPUN

GLUTLE

Yippee!

ANOTHER NAME FOR MONEY THAT'S GAINED THROUGH INHERITANCE.

Now arrange the circled letters to form the surprise answer, as suggested by the above cartoon.

Print answer here " ⬡⬡⬡⬡ – ⬡⬡⬡⬡⬡⬡ "

JUMBLE®

Unscramble these four Jumbles, one letter to each square, to form four ordinary words.

OOCCA

NIORB

DORWYB

GLOANO

WHAT THE ACCORDIONIST'S CONCERT WAS.

Now arrange the circled letters to form the surprise answer, as suggested by the above cartoon.

Print answer here ⬡⬡⬡⬡ ⬡⬡⬡⬡⬡ OUT

JUMBLE®

Unscramble these four Jumbles, one letter to each square, to form four ordinary words.

LYMIF

DALIP

DORFIL

OPPELE

Hey—how do you expect a guy to get any sleep?

WHAT THE ANGRY MUMMY DID.

Now arrange the circled letters to form the surprise answer, as suggested by the above cartoon.

Print answer here ⬡⬡⬡⬡⬡⬡⬡ HIS ⬡⬡⬡

JUMBLE®

Unscramble these four Jumbles, one letter to each square, to form four ordinary words.

TALUF

SBELS

CATATH

LOVVEE

WHY YOU MIGHT
CONSULT A
PLASTIC SURGEON.

Now arrange the circled letters to form the surprise answer, as suggested by the above cartoon.

Print answer here TO ⬡⬡⬡⬡ ⬡⬡⬡⬡

JUMBLE®

Unscramble these four Jumbles, one letter to
each square, to form four ordinary words.

VILEN

BRILO

GLEINT

WARMOR

Really! And is that
lipstick on your collar?

HOW THE POOR
FISH GOT HOOKED.

Now arrange the circled letters to form the
surprise answer, as suggested by the above
cartoon.

Print answer here WITH HIS ⬡⬡⬡ ⬡⬡⬡⬡

JUMBLE®

Unscramble these four Jumbles, one letter to each square, to form four ordinary words.

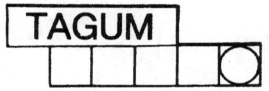

TAGUM

LULBY

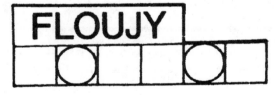

COPTEK

FLOUJY

I'm not gonna like this!

HOW THE ANESTHESIOLOGIST'S PATIENT FELT.

Now arrange the circled letters to form the surprise answer, as suggested by the above cartoon.

Print answer here VERY

JUMBLE®

Unscramble these four Jumbles, one letter to
each square, to form four ordinary words.

SMUNI

LEAGE

LINCOU

BORBEJ

HOW THE
COTTON TYCOON
FOUND HIS WORK.

Now arrange the circled letters to form the
surprise answer, as suggested by the above
cartoon.

*Print
answer
here*   VERY

JUMBLE®

Unscramble these four Jumbles, one letter to each square, to form four ordinary words.

KNUSK

TULIB

GENPOS

NAUMUT

THEY SAID
THE BACHELOR
WAS NEVER THIS.

Now arrange the circled letters to form the surprise answer, as suggested by the above cartoon.

Print answer here " ☐☐☐☐ - ☐☐☐☐☐ "

JUMBLE®

Unscramble these four Jumbles, one letter to each square, to form four ordinary words.

UPYPP

INGEF

CLUNKO

HIGLES

I need courage

HOW TO MAKE DRACULA HAPPY.

Now arrange the circled letters to form the surprise answer, as suggested by the above cartoon.

Print answer here

⬡⬡⬡⬡⬡ YOUR ⬡⬡⬡⬡⬡ ⬡⬡

JUMBLE®

Unscramble these four Jumbles, one letter to
each square, to form four ordinary words.

PURUS

ERECK

CATBUD

SWORDY

WHAT A PERSON
WHO SPENDS
TOO MUCH TIME
STUDYING CERAMICS
MIGHT END UP AS.

Now arrange the circled letters to form the
surprise answer, as suggested by the above
cartoon.

Print answer here A

JUMBLE®

Unscramble these four Jumbles, one letter to
each square, to form four ordinary words.

DONUP

UNEES

DOUSIT

SWILEY

WHAT THE YO-YO
BUSINESS HAS.

Now arrange the circled letters to form the
surprise answer, as suggested by the above
cartoon.

Print answer here ITS ☐☐☐ & ☐☐☐☐☐

JUMBLE®

Unscramble these four Jumbles, one letter to
each square, to form four ordinary words.

HOBOT

TRAIE

WEREVS

NOOMIK

Oh, well—the
pay is good

HE LIKED
THE JOB BUT
HATED THIS.

Now arrange the circled letters to form the
surprise answer, as suggested by the above
cartoon.

Print answer here

JUMBLE®

Unscramble these four Jumbles, one letter to
each square, to form four ordinary words.

DYNAD

WILLT

CLAISO

REVOUD

It's all over for me

WHAT A
GAMBLING ADDICT
USUALLY IS.

Now arrange the circled letters to form the
surprise answer, as suggested by the above
cartoon.

Print
answer   AT ⬡⬡⬡⬡ WITH ⬡⬡⬡⬡⬡
here   THE

JUMBLE®

Unscramble these four Jumbles, one letter to
each square, to form four ordinary words.

HANNE

MARRO

TOESGO

NOPPIL

THAT CONCEITED GUY
DIDN'T FEEL THE
NEED FOR A VACATION
BECAUSE HE WAS
ALREADY ON THIS.

Now arrange the circled letters to form the
surprise answer, as suggested by the above
cartoon.

Print answer here

JUMBLE®

Unscramble these four Jumbles, one letter to each square, to form four ordinary words.

RUPEN

ORNED

MESTIK

LAFTUR

Tell me more

WHAT A FLATTERER SELDOM IS.

Now arrange the circled letters to form the surprise answer, as suggested by the above cartoon.

Print answer here

JUMBLE®

Unscramble these four Jumbles, one letter to each square, to form four ordinary words.

GOUCH

ORFUR

HUMILS

YATAPH

He's stealing the show

Until now I was falling asleep

WHAT THE ACROBAT MADE A SUCCESS OF.

Now arrange the circled letters to form the surprise answer, as suggested by the above cartoon.

Print answer here

JUMBLE®

Unscramble these four Jumbles, one letter to
each square, to form four ordinary words.

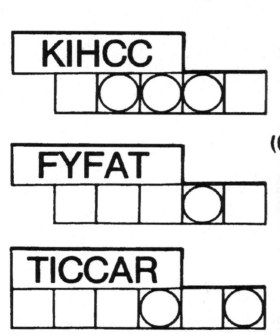

KIHCC

FYFAT

TICCAR

LARBUT

Next!

WHAT DERMATOLOGY
IS THE SCIENCE OF.

Now arrange the circled letters to form the
surprise answer, as suggested by the above
cartoon.

Print answer here

JUMBLE®

Unscramble these four Jumbles, one letter to each square, to form four ordinary words.

BELLI

VALIE

VORAYS

DULCOY

HOW THAT COMICAL SERGEANT STARTED THE DAY FOR HIS TROOPS.

Now arrange the circled letters to form the surprise answer, as suggested by the above cartoon.

Print answer here   WITH " ◯◯◯◯◯ " ◯◯◯◯

JUMBLE®

Unscramble these four Jumbles, one letter to
each square, to form four ordinary words.

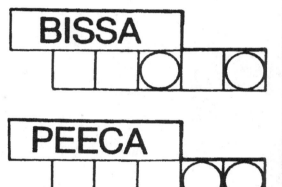

BISSA

PEECA

TURAIN

BOAMEA

WHAT THE POOREST
WAITERS IN SOME
RESTAURANTS ARE.

Now arrange the circled letters to form the
surprise answer, as suggested by the above
cartoon.

Print answer here

130

JUMBLE®

Unscramble these four Jumbles, one letter to each square, to form four ordinary words.

RIMEN

CUDIL

SULTES

GELIGG

WHAT SHE
SAID AT THE
COSTUME PARTY.

Now arrange the circled letters to form the surprise answer, as suggested by the above cartoon.

Print answer here

"⬡⬡⬡ - ⬡⬡⬡⬡⬡" FOR ⬡⬡ !

131

JUMBLE®

Unscramble these four Jumbles, one letter to each square, to form four ordinary words.

CIKHT

WREEF

STEBIC

STOLCY

Heh heh—I win the match!

HOW A HANDICAPPED GOLFER PLAYS.

Now arrange the circled letters to form the surprise answer, as suggested by the above cartoon.

Print answer here  HIS

132

JUMBLE®

Unscramble these four Jumbles, one letter to each square, to form four ordinary words.

THALC

MIGRY

CHYSIP

YAHNTS

It should be secure here

WHAT A SAFE
DEPOSIT BOX
MIGHT BE CALLED.

Now arrange the circled letters to form the surprise answer, as suggested by the above cartoon.

Print answer here A ☐☐☐☐☐ ☐☐☐☐☐

JUMBLE®

Unscramble these four Jumbles, one letter to
each square, to form four ordinary words.

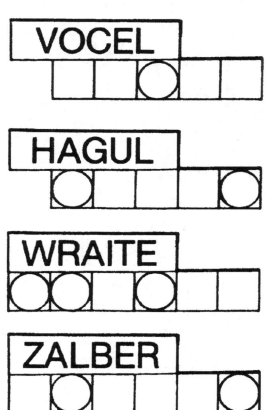

VOCEL

HAGUL

WRAITE

ZALBER

A SPENDTHRIFT
WIFE MIGHT
LOVE HER
HUSBAND FOR THIS.

Now arrange the circled letters to form the
surprise answer, as suggested by the above
cartoon.

Print answer here

JUMBLE®

Unscramble these four Jumbles, one letter to
each square, to form four ordinary words.

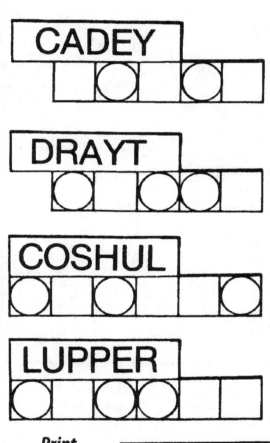

CADEY

DRAYT

COSHUL

LUPPER

WHAT AN
EASY TALKER
GENERALLY IS.

Now arrange the circled letters to form the
surprise answer, as suggested by the above
cartoon.

Print
answer A
here

JUMBLE®

Unscramble these four Jumbles, one letter to
each square, to form four ordinary words.

IPEEC

TINFE

HERTHS

MIDOWS

WHAT A GOOD
SHRINK IS
SUPPOSED TO BE.

Now arrange the circled letters to form the
surprise answer, as suggested by the above
cartoon.

*Print
answer* A
here

JUMBLE®

Unscramble these four Jumbles, one letter to each square, to form four ordinary words.

ZYCAR

EMARK

SETTAL

HESTOO

No ambition

And look at those shoes

WHAT LOAFERS LACK.

Now arrange the circled letters to form the surprise answer, as suggested by the above cartoon.

Print answer here

JUMBLE®

Unscramble these four Jumbles, one letter to each square, to form four ordinary words.

GIERT

EVIRT

DOCEED

LARPOR

FOR THAT GAMBLER, THIS WAS THE NEXT THING TO HEAVEN.

Now arrange the circled letters to form the surprise answer, as suggested by the above cartoon.

Print answer here A "◯◯◯◯◯ ◯' ◯◯◯◯"

JUMBLE®

Unscramble these four Jumbles, one letter to each square, to form four ordinary words.

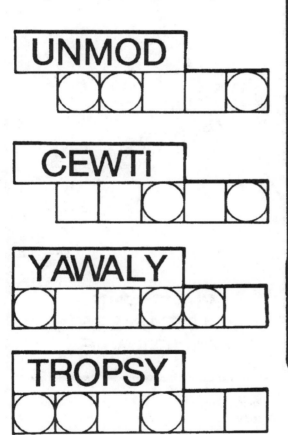

UNMOD

CEWTI

YAWALY

TROPSY

I think that one's got something to tell us

ALTHOUGH IT WON'T NECESSARILY MAKE YOU RICH, YOU MIGHT GET THIS FROM AN INTELLIGENT OYSTER.

Now arrange the circled letters to form the surprise answer, as suggested by the above cartoon.

Print answer here A ⬭⬭⬭⬭⬭ OF ⬭⬭⬭⬭⬭⬭

JUMBLE.

Unscramble these four Jumbles, one letter to
each square, to form four ordinary words.

PHOCE

INGYL

BILDOY

COYTUR

WHAT THE
MOUNTAINEER'S
MASCOT WAS.

Now arrange the circled letters to form the
surprise answer, as suggested by the above
cartoon.

Print answer here " ☐☐☐ ☐☐☐ "

JUMBLE®

Unscramble these four Jumbles, one letter to each square, to form four ordinary words.

CILRY
▢▢◯◯▢

LYKIM
▢▢◯▢▢

NESSUL
▢◯◯◯▢▢

PERMUB
▢◯◯▢◯

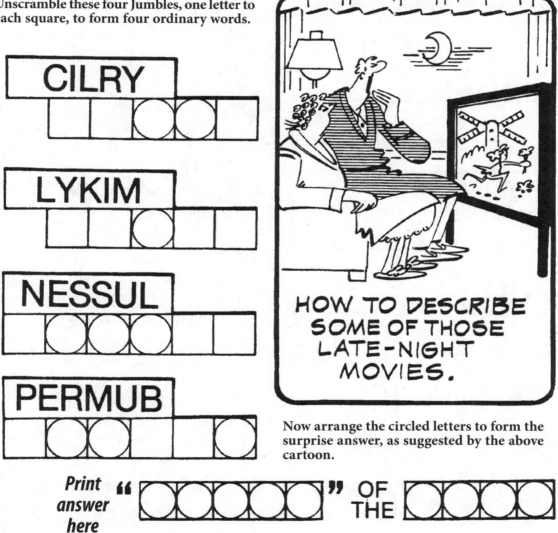

HOW TO DESCRIBE SOME OF THOSE LATE-NIGHT MOVIES.

Now arrange the circled letters to form the surprise answer, as suggested by the above cartoon.

Print answer here " ◯◯◯◯◯ " OF THE ◯◯◯◯

Unscramble these four Jumbles, one letter to
each square, to form four ordinary words.

ENZOO

WENYL

URBBUS

TOOWWK

I thought he'd never ask

HE HAD TO GIVE
HER A FAKE
DIAMOND BECAUSE
HE WAS THIS.

Now arrange the circled letters to form the
surprise answer, as suggested by the above
cartoon.

Print answer here "◯◯◯◯◯" ◯◯◯◯◯

JUMBLE®

Unscramble these four Jumbles, one letter to
each square, to form four ordinary words.

CAINP

GUDOH

DOLSUN

SARGYS

WHAT FORM
OF SPEECH
IS DOUBLE-TALK?

Now arrange the circled letters to form the
surprise answer, as suggested by the above
cartoon.

Print answer here VERY " ⬡⬡⬡⬡⬡⬡⬡⬡ "

JUMBLE®

Unscramble these four Jumbles, one letter to each square, to form four ordinary words.

AGGUE

RICLY

DUPHEL

MONFIR

SILENCE

WHAT THEY CALLED THE GENEALOGIST.

Now arrange the circled letters to form the surprise answer, as suggested by the above cartoon.

Print answer here THE "⬭⬭⬭⬭⬭" ⬭⬭⬭⬭⬭⬭⬭

JUMBLE®

Unscramble these four Jumbles, one letter to each square, to form four ordinary words.

EVING

TOAFO

NITTEK

YASILE

This is your idea of taking me out to dinner?

WHAT THEY CALLED THAT STINGY DERMATOLOGIST.

Now arrange the circled letters to form the surprise answer, as suggested by the above cartoon.

Print answer here A

JUMBLE®

Unscramble these four Jumbles, one letter to
each square, to form four ordinary words.

DYLOM

KAQUE

VEGASA

HECARB

WHAT THAT GIRL
WHO LOOKED
LIKE A MILLION
BUCKS WAS.

Now arrange the circled letters to form the
surprise answer, as suggested by the above
cartoon.

*Print
answer
here* JUST AS ◯◯◯◯ TO ◯◯◯◯

JUMBLE®

Unscramble these four Jumbles, one letter to each square, to form four ordinary words.

CAZER

NAREY

DILERB

TESHEE

Those were great times

WHAT NOSTALGIA SUMMONS UP.

Now arrange the circled letters to form the surprise answer, as suggested by the above cartoon.

Print answer here " ☐☐☐☐☐☐ — ☐☐☐☐ "

JUMBLE®

Unscramble these four Jumbles, one letter to
each square, to form four ordinary words.

BREWO

FYTHE

ENDECT

DILPIM

Another one of your
imaginary ailments?

WHAT A
HYPOCHONDRIAC'S
AFFLICTION
FREQUENTLY IS.

Now arrange the circled letters to form the
surprise answer, as suggested by the above
cartoon.

Print answer here A ☐☐☐☐☐☐☐☐☐

JUMBLE®

Unscramble these four Jumbles, one letter to each square, to form four ordinary words.

GAADE

SOUMY

NESTOL

BORCAN

WHAT HE SAID
WHEN THE JUDGE
SENTENCED HIM
TO BE HANGED.

Now arrange the circled letters to form the surprise answer, as suggested by the above cartoon.

Print answer here THAT'S ◯◯◯ " ◯◯◯◯◯ "

JUMBLE®

Unscramble these four Jumbles, one letter to
each square, to form four ordinary words.

GLUBY

HALET

GLINJE

INDOWS

WHAT NOBILITY
USUALLY IS.

Now arrange the circled letters to form the
surprise answer, as suggested by the above
cartoon.

Print answer here " ◯◯◯◯ – ◯◯◯◯◯ "

JUMBLE®

Unscramble these four Jumbles, one letter to each square, to form four ordinary words.

NUTED

RYGOL

ANGOLS

DEBUMI

HOW THAT PERFUME HELD HIM.

Now arrange the circled letters to form the surprise answer, as suggested by the above cartoon.

Print answer here "◯◯◯◯◯—◯◯◯◯◯"

JUMBLE®

Unscramble these four Jumbles, one letter to
each square, to form four ordinary words.

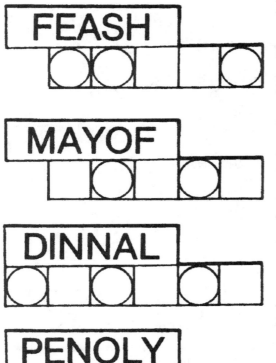

FEASH

MAYOF

DINNAL

PENOLY

He's very
conceited

WHAT THE
EGOTISTICAL
NUDIST WAS ALL
WRAPPED UP IN.

Now arrange the circled letters to form the
surprise answer, as suggested by the above
cartoon.

*Print
answer
here*

JUMBLE®

Unscramble these four Jumbles, one letter to each square, to form four ordinary words.

SHECS

HIRMT

DREHWS

TIPIDE

WHAT A MINISKIRT IS.

Now arrange the circled letters to form the surprise answer, as suggested by the above cartoon.

Print answer here A " ⬡⬡⬡⬡⬡ - ⬡⬡⬡⬡⬡ "

JUMBLE®

Unscramble these four Jumbles, one letter to
each square, to form four ordinary words.

CULOT

LAMBY

LESING

TREBUT

WHAT YOU NEED
TO HAVE IN
ORDER TO BE AN
ORGAN GRINDER.

Now arrange the circled letters to form the
surprise answer, as suggested by the above
cartoon.

Print
answer A ⬡⬡⬡⬡⬡ FOR ⬡⬡⬡⬡⬡⬡
here

JUMBLE®

Unscramble these four Jumbles, one letter to each square, to form four ordinary words.

OCTEM

HIWGE

ENOMAY

GAUHTT

Can't make the sauce without it

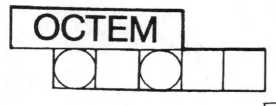

WHY THE COOK HURRIED TO THE HERB GARDEN.

Now arrange the circled letters to form the surprise answer, as suggested by the above cartoon.

Print answer here   HE HADN'T ⬚⬚⬚⬚ " ⬚⬚⬚⬚⬚ "

JUMBLE®

Unscramble these four Jumbles, one letter to
each square, to form four ordinary words.

USEED

DAHYN

CAPELA

BOREEF

WHAT THE INTELLI-
GENCE AGENT HAD
WHEN HE STAYED
HOME FROM WORK.

Now arrange the circled letters to form the
surprise answer, as suggested by the above
cartoon.

Print answer here A " ◯◯◯◯◯ " IN THE ◯◯◯◯◯

JUMBLE®

Unscramble these four Jumbles, one letter to
each square, to form four ordinary words.

LOBAT

TYMPE

SHAPIR

POMSIE

WHAT THE TREE
THAT EVERYONE
GATHERED UNDER
WAS CALLED.

Now arrange the circled letters to form the
surprise answer, as suggested by the above
cartoon.

Print answer here " ⬡⬡⬡ ' ⬡⬡⬡ "

JUMBLE®

Unscramble these four Jumbles, one letter to each square, to form four ordinary words.

VEYHA

THOUY

SULTES

INDOWS

HIS APTITUDE FOR PLATITUDE CREATES THIS IN HIS AUDIENCE.

Now arrange the circled letters to form the surprise answer, as suggested by the above cartoon.

Print answer here

JUMBLE®

Unscramble these four Jumbles, one letter to
each square, to form four ordinary words.

MORRA

CNOTH

LOWALT

DEEMLY

You're gorgeous!

Harold!

WOMEN DETEST FLAT-
TERY, ESPECIALLY
WHEN IT'S DIRECTED
TOWARD THIS.

Now arrange the circled letters to form the
surprise answer, as suggested by the above
cartoon.

Print answer here

JUMBLE®

Unscramble these four Jumbles, one letter to each square, to form four ordinary words.

ALZEH

BOMIL

LAUTAC

NERRED

I don't see any bargains here

Looks like a rip-off to me

A FIRE SALE IS A PLACE WHERE BARGAIN HUNTERS MIGHT GET THIS.

Now arrange the circled letters to form the surprise answer, as suggested by the above cartoon.

Print answer here " ◯◯◯◯◯◯ "

JUMBLE®

Unscramble these four Jumbles, one letter to
each square, to form four ordinary words.

NOCIT

TONJI

PAICEE

RISDAM

SOME PEOPLE WHO
THINK THEY'RE
"OPERATING" IN THE
STOCK MARKET ARE
SOMETIMES THIS.

Now arrange the circled letters to form the
surprise answer, as suggested by the above
cartoon.

Print
answer
here   " ⬡⬡⬡⬡⬡⬡⬡⬡⬡ ⬡⬡ "

JUMBLE®

Unscramble these four Jumbles, one letter to
each square, to form four ordinary words.

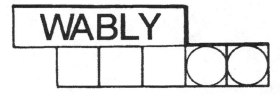

WABLY

DAPAT

NAWKEE

REBUPS

Stocks went down, and it
looks like rain

THE PESSIMIST HAD
A HAPPY LOOK EVERY
TIME HE HAD THIS
TO REPORT.

Now arrange the circled letters to form the
surprise answer, as suggested by the above
cartoon.

Print answer here

JUMBLE®

Juggernaut

Challenger Puzzles

JUMBLE®

Unscramble these six Jumbles, one letter to each square, to form six ordinary words.

CHUNAH

MOONID

YAMSIL

URRUMM

SCIBEP

DANNEC

You're not too smart

Says who?

FOUND AT A VENTRILOQUISTS' CONVENTION.

Now arrange the circled letters to form the surprise answer, as suggested by the above cartoon.

Print answer here

A ⟨◯◯◯◯◯⟩ OF ⟨◯◯◯◯◯◯◯◯⟩

JUMBLE®

Unscramble these six Jumbles, one letter to each square, to form six ordinary words.

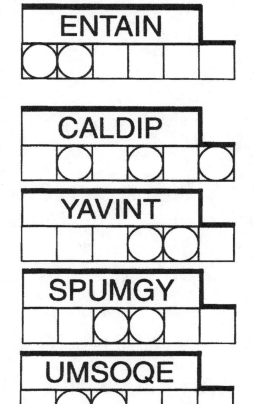

ENTAIN

CALDIP

YAVINT

SPUMGY

UMSOQE

SIPCLE

I'm taking
the house
and the car

WHAT THE BOXER
GOT WHEN HIS
WIFE DECIDED TO
FILE FOR DIVORCE.

Now arrange the circled letters to form the surprise answer, as suggested by the above cartoon.

Print answer here

A " ⃝⃝⃝⃝⃝ " ⃝⃝⃝⃝⃝⃝⃝⃝

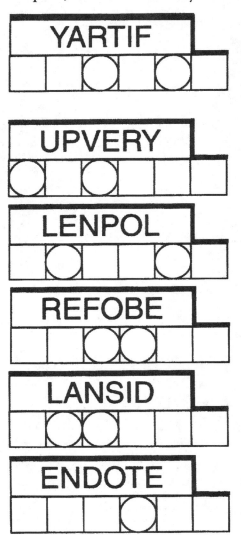

JUMBLE®

Unscramble these six Jumbles, one letter to each square, to form six ordinary words.

YARTIF

UPVERY

LENPOL

REFOBE

LANSID

ENDOTE

C'mon, Joe, you can do it

They support each other

WHAT SWIMMERS DO TO WIN A RELAY RACE.

Now arrange the circled letters to form the surprise answer, as suggested by the above cartoon.

Print answer here

" ⬡⬡⬡⬡ " THEIR ⬡⬡⬡⬡⬡⬡⬡⬡

JUMBLE®

Unscramble these six Jumbles, one letter to each square, to form six ordinary words.

BOAMEA

LOVENC

FIURAN

GREDLE

RAJAUG

HYGNID

No, not going any place in particular

WHAT THE CELL PHONE USER CALLED THE HIGHWAY TOLL.

Now arrange the circled letters to form the surprise answer, as suggested by the above cartoon.

Print answer here

A

JUMBLE®

Unscramble these six Jumbles, one letter to
each square, to form six ordinary words.

BENTRA

INQUAT

MECION

COPLIE

UMPAKE

MULVLE

I'll have this
fixed in no time

WHAT HE NEEDED
TO DO WHEN HIS
LINE BROKE.

Now arrange the circled letters to form the
surprise answer, as suggested by the above
cartoon.

Print answer here

" ⬡⬡⬡⬡⬡⬡ " THE ⬡⬡⬡⬡⬡⬡⬡

JUMBLE®

Unscramble these six Jumbles, one letter to each square, to form six ordinary words.

LAWVOA

GREEME

YOUGLE

LEMETH

GEPPIN

REBARN

He's a hard worker and he learns fast

THE ELECTRICIAN GAVE THIS REGARDING HIS YOUNG APPRENTICE.

Now arrange the circled letters to form the surprise answer, as suggested by the above cartoon.

Print answer here

A " ⬡⬡⬡⬡⬡⬡⬡ " ⬡⬡⬡⬡⬡⬡

JUMBLE®

Unscramble these six Jumbles, one letter to each square, to form six ordinary words.

LEVVET

SHELIC

CAYGEN

USDABE

MANDET

NACAMI

Try developing slower, and more light

POSITIVE THINKING CAN LEAD TO THIS IN A DARKROOM.

Now arrange the circled letters to form the surprise answer, as suggested by the above cartoon.

Print answer here

" ◯◯◯◯◯◯◯ " ◯◯◯◯◯

JUMBLE®

Unscramble these six Jumbles, one letter to each square, to form six ordinary words.

DEFLAB

DUNTIC

CENTED

NIXFIG

DEMIPE

TRENGY

Don't let them stray

Let's not get cheated

A HERDER MIGHT FEAR THIS WHEN TAKING HIS SHEEP TO MARKET.

Now arrange the circled letters to form the surprise answer, as suggested by the above cartoon.

Print answer here

JUMBLE®

Unscramble these six Jumbles, one letter to
each square, to form six ordinary words.

JEGLIG

HOTFRY

DELUVA

JOBTEC

THORPY

STENOX

We're at forty fathoms

I knew we'd find it

WHAT SUCCESSFUL
DIVERS HAVE.

Now arrange the circled letters to form the
surprise answer, as suggested by the above
cartoon.

Print answer here

"  "

JUMBLE®

Unscramble these six Jumbles, one letter to each square, to form six ordinary words.

HOMIDS

EATREA

GRACIT

ALBBED

TARMIN

RAGETT

WHERE DO HIGH-
RANKING
OFFICERS SHOP?

Now arrange the circled letters to form the surprise answer, as suggested by the above cartoon.

Print answer here

AT THE " ⬡⬡⬡⬡⬡⬡⬡ " ⬡⬡⬡⬡⬡

JUMBLE®

Unscramble these six Jumbles, one letter to each square, to form six ordinary words.

CINDIT

TUNESA

LABBUE

HONGIM

CEVIED

SYTRUT

No! No! Let's put the horns over here

WHAT THE ORCHESTRA PLAYED WHEN THE NEW CONDUCTOR ARRIVED.

Now arrange the circled letters to form the surprise answer, as suggested by the above cartoon.

Print answer here

JUMBLE®

Unscramble these six Jumbles, one letter to
each square, to form six ordinary words.

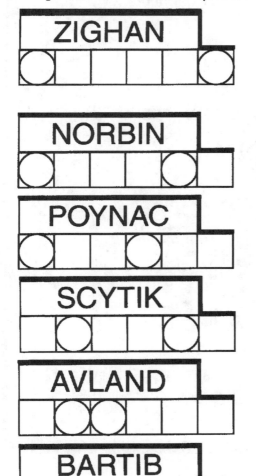

ZIGHAN

NORBIN

POYNAC

SCYTIK

AVLAND

BARTIB

These look like
deer prints

Let's
follow
them

WHEN HE WENT
HUNTING, THE
CONDUCTOR
WANTED TO
GET—

Now arrange the circled letters to form the
surprise answer, as suggested by the above
cartoon.

Print answer here

○○ THE ○○○○○ "○○○○○"

JUMBLE®

Unscramble these six Jumbles, one letter to
each square, to form six ordinary words.

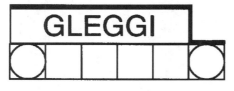

GLEGGI

SNEFTA

GLEPED

RAWSEN

DAHBEE

CEXIES

We'll get more bonuses, fewer hours ...

WHAT THE UNION
BOSS PROMISED
THE JANITORS.

Now arrange the circled letters to form the
surprise answer, as suggested by the above
cartoon.

Print answer here

JUMBLE®

Unscramble these six Jumbles, one letter to
each square, to form six ordinary words.

INKIIB

LESPEN

TAUBEY

TOORRA

TENOPT

TISSIN

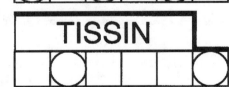

He's worth waiting for

You're right

WHAT THE DOCTOR
FOUND IN HIS
CROWDED WAITING
ROOM.

Now arrange the circled letters to form the
surprise answer, as suggested by the above
cartoon.

Print answer here

177

JUMBLE®

Unscramble these six Jumbles, one letter to
each square, to form six ordinary words.

ZARABA

THRENE

REDOAF

LIVONI

RECHOM

MILTEG

I can always
count on lefty

WHAT THE MANAGER
CONSIDERED THE
DEPENDABLE
SOUTHPAW.

Now arrange the circled letters to form the
surprise answer, as suggested by the above
cartoon.

Print answer here

HIS " ◯◯◯◯◯ ◯◯◯◯◯ " ◯◯◯

178

JUMBLE®

Unscramble these six Jumbles, one letter to
each square, to form six ordinary words.

YERMOM

COYJEK

TEECIX

HUGONE

TRUJIS

RUZZEB

WHAT SHE CON-
SIDERED HER
SCULPTURE.

Now arrange the circled letters to form the
surprise answer, as suggested by the above
cartoon.

Print answer here

A " ◯◯◯◯◯◯ " ◯◯◯◯◯◯◯◯

JUMBLE®

Unscramble these six Jumbles, one letter to each square, to form six ordinary words.

YARPIC

LUTTOE

LYBBAF

JUINER

CAUVIN

CONDES

Now arrange the circled letters to form the surprise answer, as suggested by the above cartoon.

Print answer here

THE ⬯⬯⬯⬯⬯ " ⬯⬯⬯⬯⬯⬯⬯⬯ "

JUMBLE®

Unscramble these six Jumbles, one letter to each square, to form six ordinary words.

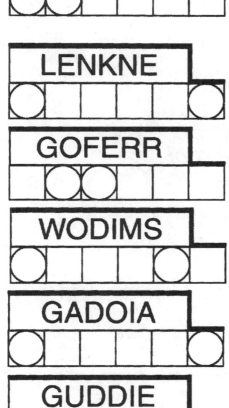

ONNIGG

LENKNE

GOFERR

WODIMS

GADOIA

GUDDIE

I've got tuition for the kids and in five years ...

IMPORTANT FOR A TRUCKER TO DO WHEN HE THINKS ABOUT THE FUTURE.

Now arrange the circled letters to form the surprise answer, as suggested by the above cartoon.

Print answer here

THE

JUMBLE®

Unscramble these six Jumbles, one letter to each square, to form six ordinary words.

SEBIED

BAYTER

GHALEG

COTIMA

SNUFUG

RAYTLE

WOW!

He works out 16 hours a day

A JUMPER WILL DO THIS TO BECOME AN OLYMPIC STAR.

Now arrange the circled letters to form the surprise answer, as suggested by the above cartoon.

Print answer here

◯◯ TO ◯◯◯◯◯◯ ◯◯◯◯◯◯◯◯

JUMBLE®

Unscramble these six Jumbles, one letter to
each square, to form six ordinary words.

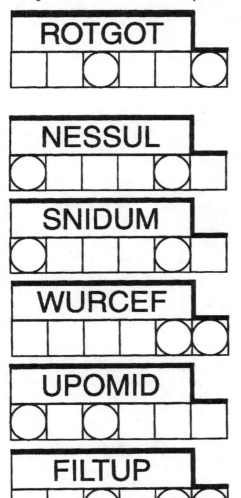

ROTGOT

NESSUL

SNIDUM

WURCEF

UPOMID

FILTUP

My horse didn't win, but it
kept my mind off food

WHAT THE
DIETING BRITON
DID AT THE
RACETRACK.

Now arrange the circled letters to form the
surprise answer, as suggested by the above
cartoon.

Print answer here

A

Answers

1. **Jumbles:** LITHE ARBOR BEHIND OUTING
   Answer: Where are some of those yuppies running?—INTO DEBT

2. **Jumbles:** BRASS MERCY SNITCH UPHELD
   Answer: If a man married a woman with a title of nobility, what would he be called?—HER HUSBAND

3. **Jumbles:** BOOTH OWING UNHOLY FERVID
   Answer: Apparently the easiest habits to break are the ones that are this—GOOD FOR YOU

4. **Jumbles:** DRYLY JUICY UNPACK BROGUE
   Answer: What you might do when you read a good horror story—"CURDLE" UP WITH IT

5. **Jumbles:** IGLOO DITTO BEDECK JITNEY
   Answer: What the inmates called their library—THE BOOKIE JOINT

6. **Jumbles:** BORAX LEAFY DEAFEN EXODUS
   Answer: He was told to eat more seafood, so now he eats every time he does this—SEE FOOD

7. **Jumbles:** MAJOR VOCAL TRUISM PALATE
   Answer: The sum total of our national debt is this—"SOME TOTAL!"

8. **Jumbles:** CLOTH SAUTE WHITEN AROUSE
   Answer: They kept minutes at the meeting but managed to do this—WASTE HOURS

9. **Jumbles:** PANIC YIELD HALLOW FESTAL
   Answer: If you don't want your dog to get run over, buy him this—A NEW "LEASH" ON LIFE

10. **Jumbles:** PROVE ROBOT QUARRY MARMOT
    Answer: What all that gossip at the boarding house amounted to—ROOMER RUMOR

11. **Jumbles:** PAGAN WOMEN SEPTIC LADING
    Answer: What he said when he bought her that new bikini—IT'S THE LEAST I CAN DO

12. **Jumbles:** CROAK YEARN QUORUM ANYHOW
    Answer: What do doctors take to get rid of the flu?—YOUR MONEY

13. **Jumbles:** TEPID FRAME PICNIC CASHEW
    Answer: She robbed her husband of his peace of mind by constantly giving him this—A PIECE OF HERS

14. **Jumbles:** UTTER WAFER THRUSH FIZZLE
    Answer: At a bargain counter this is what you get—WHAT YOU "SEIZE" (SEES)

15. **Jumbles:** LOGIC PRINT UNCOIL STYMIE
    Answer: Some politicians could help their country more by getting this—OUT OF POLITICS

16. **Jumbles:** WIPED ABYSS FECUND MAGPIE
    Answer: How to open your mouth in a way that might make others shut theirs—YAWN

17. **Jumbles:** WHINE TAKEN QUAINT PUSHER
    Answer: A few of those cheeses have this—QUITE A "PHEW"

18. **Jumbles:** WAGER CHOKE FLORAL TAWDRY
    Answer: What a bird dog might be trained for hunting in—"FOWL" WEATHER

19. **Jumbles:** ARDOR CHAIR BLUING IMPUGN
    Answer: That stingy golfer left the caddie this—HOLDING THE BAG

20. **Jumbles:** FOAMY VOUCH DEBATE ASTRAY
    Answer: A crustacean is another creature that might have this—A CRAB FOR A MATE

21. **Jumbles:** CAKED WEDGE BISECT HEREBY
    Answer: This key has been known to unlock the tongue—"WHIS-KEY"

22. **Jumbles:** SQUAB CHAOS BELFRY UNIQUE
    Answer: One woman's hobby might be another woman's this—HUBBY

23. **Jumbles:** EXPEL MUSIC LIKELY STUDIO
    Answer: Runs across the floor although it can't walk—SPILLED MILK

24. **Jumbles:** SORRY LATCH BECKON PUDDLE
    Answer: What David decided to do when Goliath started looking tired—"ROCK" HIM TO SLEEP

25. **Jumbles:** BARON NIECE SYLVAN POROUS
    Answer: "What kind of marks did you get in physical education?"—ONLY A FEW BRUISES

26. **Jumbles:** OBESE BUSHY HAMMER INTACT
    Answer: If horseback riding becomes an "addiction," this can be expensive—THE "HABIT"

27. **Jumbles:** TWILL GUILD BEGONE HORROR
    Answer: The groom was fit to be tied…DOWN

28. **Jumbles:** GUISE POUND KNIGHT EXEMPT
    Answer: Their involvement with diving was only this—SKIN DEEP

29. **Jumbles:** DROOP PURGE NORMAL UNFAIR
    Answer: A theater owner never suffers in this—THE "LONG RUN"

30. **Jumbles:** CEASE LIMIT CATNIP RANCOR
    Answer: What those old-fashioned stockyards used to have about them—A CERTAIN "AIR"

31. **Jumbles:** TRULY SWOON BEHALF INLAND
    Answer: What many dry speeches are—ALL WET

32. **Jumbles:** UNIFY TWEAK COHORT NUDISM
    Answer: Think before you speak. Then…YOU WON'T

33. **Jumbles:** AHEAD BURST PEPTIC HANDED
    Answer: The doctor said the patient's heart was this—OFF THE "BEATIN'" PATH

34. **Jumbles:** DOGMA TARDY ACHING PESTLE
    Answer: The best weight lifters—CALORIES

35. **Jumbles:** PUPIL CABIN GASKET BUCKET
    Answer: When all is said and done, some people just do this—KEEP ON TALKING

36. **Jumbles:** CHUTE SWOOP DAHLIA THEORY
    Answer: He's the "master" in his own home just so long as he does this—WHAT HE'S TOLD

37. **Jumbles:** AGENT SCOUT WINTRY HAWKER
    Answer: Money can be lost in more this—WAYS THAN "WON"

38. **Jumbles:** AVAIL TRAIT BANGLE COMEDY
    Answer: They said the movie had a happy ending because everyone was this—GLAD IT WAS OVER

39. **Jumbles:** DINER MADAM GIGGLE ORPHAN
    Answer: What that eccentric door-to-door salesman must have been—A "DING-DONG"

40. **Jumbles:** CURVE WALTZ SLUICE OBTUSE
    Answer: He dines with the upper set and is apt to do this, too—USE HIS LOWERS

41. **Jumbles:** GRAIN MOUTH DOUBLE HITHER
    Answer: What the guy who was her "ideal" became after they got married—HER ORDEAL

42. **Jumbles:** HOVEL GUIDE SAFARI TURTLE
    Answer: Why he took the screens off his windows—TO LET THE FLIES OUT

43. **Jumbles:** PUPPY FEVER BEAGLE ENSIGN
    Answer: The only time that crook's on the level is when he's this—SLEEPING

44. **Jumbles:** BARGE AZURE DABBLE YELLOW
    Answer: He wanted to become a lawyer badly, but he ended up becoming this—A BAD LAWYER

45. **Jumbles:** PERKY JOLLY GRASSY ELEVEN
    Answer: Any man who argues with his wife and wins…LOSES

46. **Jumbles:** IVORY EIGHT WEEVIL TANDEM
    Answer: When you "live it up," you might try to do this afterward—LIVE IT DOWN

47. **Jumbles:** STOOP BRIBE DRAGON SURTAX
    Answer: Dipping your bread into gravy may be bad manners, but it's certainly also this—"GOOD TASTE"

48. **Jumbles:** ARRAY GAVEL EMBODY VERSUS
    Answer: A man who claims he never makes a mistake isn't this—VERY BUSY

49. **Jumbles:** TEMPO ABATE GUITAR SPLEEN
    Answer: A bikini never attracts attention until someone does this—PUTS IT ON

50. **Jumbles:** GOOSE AMUSE SAVORY BUSHEL
    Answer: In these very words he told his wife who the boss was—"YOU'RE THE BOSS!"

51. **Jumbles:** AUDIT DECRY ENMITY BARROW
    Answer: That lonely guy robbed a bank just so he could feel this—"WANTED"

52. **Jumbles:** GUMBO BRIAR FORKED CROTCH
    Answer: She can dish it out, but can she do this?—COOK IT

53. **Jumbles:** MIDGE AUGUR DISCUS GENTLE
    Answer: When they reach middle age, many people are reduced to this—REDUCING

54. **Jumbles:** COACH ANKLE NUTRIA DEVOUR
    Answer: The best way to tell a woman's age is when she's this—NOT AROUND

55. **Jumbles:** SNOWY CATCH INLAID GYRATE
    Answer: How the miser got rich—THE "HOARD" WAY

56. **Jumbles:** THINK VIXEN MYSELF SAFARI
    Answer: What the fisherman's gross income was—SAME AS HIS "NET"

57. **Jumbles:** AISLE COACH FORGER DURESS
    Answer: What that math whiz who rose to the top of the firm ended up as—THE FIGUREHEAD

58. **Jumbles:** HANDY AMUSE YELLOW DISCUS
    Answer: What the highway maintenance man was told to do—MEND HIS "WAY"

59. **Jumbles:** FLAKE BLOOM FUTURE TONGUE
    Answer: How to silence a "loud" tie—GET A "MUFFLER"

60. **Jumbles:** HURRY BISON GRATIS FORKED
    Answer: What the professional crap-shooter's business must have been—"SHAKY"

61. **Jumbles:** WHEAT DAILY SUGARY FIRING
    Answer: The horse you put your money on often does this—RUNS AWAY WITH IT

62. **Jumbles:** ABASH CHANT MISLAY UNFOLD
    Answer: A stubborn man doesn't hold opinions…THEY HOLD HIM

63. **Jumbles:** MAIZE ALIVE QUAVER FIESTA
    Answer: In addition to money, the rich never seem to lack this—RELATIVES

64. **Jumbles:** PYLON TWEET EXHALE DIGEST
    Answer: What the sentry at the army kitchen kept—HIS EYES "PEELED"

65. **Jumbles:** DRAMA BASIN STOOGE UNEASY
    Answer: Is she a good dressmaker?—SO IT "SEAMS"

66. **Jumbles:** NEEDY DUNCE FITFUL CHROME
    Answer: He was a friend of the owner, which is why he got everything…ON THE "CUFF"

67. **Jumbles:** CHAMP BUILT KILLER POETRY
    Answer: What they called those two porcupines—A PRICKLY "PAIR"

68. **Jumbles:** GNOME JOUST MAKEUP SAVAGE
    Answer: Sticks to one thing and hopefully gets there—A STAMP

69. **Jumbles:** ODIUM BANJO CIRCUS HAPPEN
    Answer: What to tie up that grand with—PIANO "CHORDS"

70. **Jumbles:** GROIN HYENA KITTEN RECTOR
    Answer: They've improved the trains to Washington so that the politicians can now do this—GET ON THE RIGHT TRACK

71. **Jumbles:** BEGOT ENSUE NEARBY RADIUM
    Answer: She used to be afraid of mice until she finally decided to do this—MARRY ONE

72. **Jumbles:** WHILE AFTER BUSILY AMBUSH
    Answer: What's the underground movement that's going on in many cities?—THE SUBWAY

73. **Jumbles:** KITTY BAGGY TURNIP MATURE
    Answer: One sure way to beat the stock market—JUST "BEAT IT!"

74. **Jumbles:** LEAVE PAUSE FERRET HARROW
    Answer: What a rainy day is for a cab driver—"FARE" WEATHER

75. **Jumbles:** VALET HURRY UPWARD SUBMIT
    Answer: The pessimist was hanging around the delicatessen store because he was waiting for this—THE "WURST"

76. **Jumbles:** BEFIT PUTTY HEAVEN FALLOW
    Answer: What a good police dog might put—TEETH INTO THE LAW

77. **Jumbles:** DOUSE BLOOD LEEWAY RATIFY
    Answer: Every time he has an argument with his wife, this happens—WORDS "FLAIL" HIM

78. **Jumbles:** STOKE AIDED CENSUS SOLACE
    Answer: What the ship's doctors generally do—"SEE SICKNESS"

79. **Jumbles:** FORAY SYLPH UNLOAD LARYNX
    Answer: If you become addicted to wrestling, it might do this—GET A HOLD ON YOU

80. **Jumbles:** GRIEF HOUSE TOTTER NUANCE
    Answer: He married a rich wife, so he never had to pay anything…except this—ATTENTION

81. **Jumbles:** GRAVE POKED BUTTER SOCIAL
    Answer: What the canine member of the Boy Scouts was called—A "BEAGLE" SCOUT

82. **Jumbles:** ITCHY KETCH FIGURE TACKLE
    Answer: He thought he was a wit, and most of them said he was this—HALF RIGHT

83. **Jumbles:** BLANK WRATH AGENCY JOSTLE
    Answer: What the robber tried to do after he stole all the money—"STEAL" AWAY

84. **Jumbles:** THINK POWER JURIST SCURVY
    Answer: "Does your wife pick your clothes?"—"JUST THE POCKETS"

85. **Jumbles:** VIPER NOISY PEPSIN LICHEN
    Answer: He tried to kiss her, but she'd have this—NONE OF HIS LIP

86. **Jumbles:** BASIC QUILT MELODY CARPET
    Answer: What lace should never be—OUT OF "P-LACE"

87. **Jumbles:** RIGOR NEWSY GENIUS RARITY
    Answer: Bigamy is when two—"RITES" MAKE A WRONG

88. **Jumbles:** DEMON RUSTY SKEWER FETISH
    Answer: When you try to wash a small kid, he's apt to do this—SHRINK FROM IT

89. **Jumbles:** UNITY SCOUR BAKING CAMPER
    Answer: Some aging thespians might find it difficult to do this—ACT THEIR AGE

90. **Jumbles:** ERUPT HELLO UNSAID RARELY
    Answer: One way to get ahead and stay ahead is to do this—USE YOUR HEAD

91. **Jumbles:** BOGUS QUASH MUSKET CLERGY
    Answer: What legal "tender" might be when you don't have it—"TOUGH"

92. **Jumbles:** HUSKY AGILE BEAUTY IMBIBE
    Answer: In those days a woman would raise a hem in order to do this—GET A "HIM"

93. **Jumbles:** AORTA CARGO POWDER JUNIOR
Answer: Another name for a cloudburst—
A "DROWN POUR"

94. **Jumbles:** JUMBO TOXIC SCORCH PIRACY
Answer: Something often found in newspapers and on beaches—A COMIC "STRIP"

95. **Jumbles:** FATAL DIZZY INFORM PITIED
Answer: A surgeon might have to cut out something because the patient this—DID NOT

96. **Jumbles:** MANLY BILGE FLAXEN CASKET
Answer: Most people are put out when they're this—"TAKEN IN"

97. **Jumbles:** VENOM MESSY SHREWD OUTLET
Answer: What do you get when a monster steps on a house?—"MUSHED ROOMS"

98. **Jumbles:** JEWEL BLIMP DARING POUNCE
Answer: What a marriage certificate should be written on—"BOND" PAPER

99. **Jumbles:** LEAKY BURLY EYEFUL VISION
Answer: What were the shoemaker's two favorite kinds of fish?—SOLE AND 'EEL (heel)

100. **Jumbles:** BULLY GIANT SONATA DEMURE
Answer: He promised first that he would be this—TRUE TO THE LAST

101. **Jumbles:** BEIGE HASTY STUCCO PAROLE
Answer: A pea-soupy fog may give motorists this—THE "CREEPS"

102. **Jumbles:** FOCUS MAGIC HARBOR GHETTO
Answer: Might also be "fired"…even when seemingly this—A BIG "SHOT"

103. **Jumbles:** SOAPY MAUVE FROTHY TRIPLE
Answer: The younger generation always seems more outrageous when one is no longer this—A PART OF IT

104. **Jumbles:** LOFTY THICK SADIST PILLAR
Answer: What he got as a result of careless driving—A "LIP LASH"

105. **Jumbles:** FLOUR TOPAZ WHEEZE HALVED
Answer: That wiseacre has the solution to every difficult problem right in this—THE HOLLOW OF HIS HEAD

106. **Jumbles:** CRAZE ABIDE TYPIST BLOUSE
Answer: What ignorance at the beach is—"BLISS-TER"

107. **Jumbles:** HOARD PIKER TONGUE INHALE
Answer: Why the burlesque queen decided to run for office—SHE HAD NOTHING TO HIDE

108. **Jumbles:** DOILY JUROR VIOLIN PHYSIC
Answer: What happens every time he turns over a new leaf?—IT'S POISON IVY

109. **Jumbles:** BRAVE COLON DELUGE ADAGIO
Answer: This might help a gambler win a good deal of chips—A GOOD DEAL

110. **Jumbles:** NOVEL MINUS UPTOWN GULLET
Answer: Another name for money that's gained through inheritance—"WILL-GOTTEN"

111. **Jumbles:** COCOA ROBIN BYWORD LAGOON
Answer: What the accordionist's concert was—LONG DRAWN OUT

112. **Jumbles:** FILMY PLAID FLORID PEOPLE
Answer: What the angry mummy did—FLIPPED HIS LID

113. **Jumbles:** FAULT BLESS ATTACH EVOLVE
Answer: Why you might consult a plastic surgeon—TO SAVE FACE

114. **Jumbles:** LIVEN BROIL TINGLE MARROW
Answer: How the poor fish got hooked—WITH HIS OWN LINE

115. **Jumbles:** GAMUT BULLY POCKET JOYFUL
Answer: How the anesthesiologist's patient felt—VERY "PUT OUT"

116. **Jumbles:** MINUS EAGLE UNCOIL JOBBER
Answer: How the cotton tycoon found his work—VERY ABSORBING

117. **Jumbles:** SKUNK BUILT SPONGE AUTUMN
Answer: They said the bachelor was never this—"MISS-TAKEN"

118. **Jumbles:** PUPPY FEIGN UNLOCK SLEIGH
Answer: How to make Dracula happy—KEEP YOUR CHIN UP

119. **Jumbles:** USURP CREEK ABDUCT DROWSY
Answer: What a person who spends too much time studying ceramics might end up as—A CRACKPOT

120. **Jumbles:** POUND ENSUE STUDIO WISELY
Answer: What the yo-yo business has—ITS UPS & DOWNS

121. **Jumbles:** BOOTH IRATE SWERVE KIMONO
Answer: He liked the job but hated this—THE WORK

122. **Jumbles:** DANDY TWILL SOCIAL DEVOUR
Answer: What a gambling addict usually is—AT ODDS WITH THE WORLD

123. **Jumbles:** HENNA ARMOR STOOGE POPLIN
Answer: That conceited guy didn't feel the need for a vacation because he was already on this—AN EGO TRIP

124. **Jumbles:** PRUNE DRONE KISMET ARTFUL
Answer: What a flatterer seldom is—INTERRUPTED

125. **Jumbles:** COUGH FUROR MULISH APATHY
Answer: What the acrobat made a success of—A "FLOP"

126. **Jumbles:** CHICK TAFFY ARCTIC BRUTAL
Answer: What dermatology is the science of—"ITCH CRAFT"

127. **Jumbles:** LIBEL ALIVE SAVORY CLOUDY
Answer: How that comical sergeant started the day for his troops—WITH "DROLL" CALL

128. **Jumbles:** BASIS PEACE NUTRIA AMOEBA
Answer: What the poorest waiters in some restaurants are—CUSTOMERS

129. **Jumbles:** MINER LUCID TUSSLE GIGGLE
Answer: What she said at the costume party—"DIS-GUISE" FOR ME! (This guy's for me)

130. **Jumbles:** THICK FEWER BISECT COSTLY
Answer: How a handicapped golfer plays—WITH HIS BOSS

131. **Jumbles:** LATCH GRIMY PHYSIC SHANTY
Answer: What a safe deposit box might be called—A RICH NITCH

132. **Jumbles:** CLOVE LAUGH WAITER BLAZER
Answer: A spendthrift wife might love her husband for this—ALL HE'S WORTH

133. **Jumbles:** DECAY TARDY SLOUCH PURPLE
Answer: What an easy talker generally is—A HARD STOPPER

134. **Jumbles:** PIECE FEINT THRESH WISDOM
Answer: What a good shrink is supposed to be—A MIND SWEEPER

135. **Jumbles:** CRAZY MAKER LATEST SOOTHE
Answer: What loafers lack—SHOELACES

136. **Jumbles:** TIGER RIVET DECODE PARLOR
Answer: For that gambler, this was the next thing to heaven—A "PAIR O' DICE" (paradise)

137. **Jumbles:** MOUND TWICE WAYLAY SPORTY
Answer: Although it won't necessarily make you rich, you might get this from an intelligent oyster—A PEARL OF WISDOM

138. **Jumbles:** EPOCH LYING BODILY OUTCRY
Answer: What the mountaineer's mascot was—"TOP DOG"

139. **Jumbles:** LYRIC MILKY UNLESS BUMPER
Answer: How to describe some of those late-night movies—"RERUN" OF THE MILL

140. **Jumbles:** OZONE NEWLY SUBURB KOWTOW
Answer: He had to give her a fake diamond because he was this—"STONE" BROKE

141. **Jumbles:** PANIC DOUGH UNSOLD GRASSY
Answer: What form of speech is double-talk?—VERY "SINGULAR"

142. **Jumbles:** GAUGE LYRIC UPHELD INFORM
Answer: What they called the genealogist—THE "CLAN" DIGGER

143. **Jumbles:** GIVEN AFOOT KITTEN EASILY
Answer: What they called that stingy dermatologist—A SKINFLINT

144. **Jumbles:** MOLDY QUAKE SAVAGE BREACH
Answer: What that girl who looked like a million bucks was—JUST AS HARD TO MAKE

145. **Jumbles:** CRAZE YEARN BRIDLE SEETHE
Answer: What nostalgia summons up—"YESTER-DAZE"

146. **Jumbles:** BOWER HEFTY DECENT LIMPID
Answer: What a hypochondriac's affliction frequently is—A FICTION

147. **Jumbles:** ADAGE MOUSY STOLEN CARBON
Answer: What he said when the judge sentenced him to be hanged—THAT'S BAD "NOOSE"

148. **Jumbles:** BULGY LATHE JINGLE DISOWN
Answer: What nobility usually is—"SNOB-ILITY"

149. **Jumbles:** TUNED GLORY SLOGAN IMBUED
Answer: How that perfume held him—"SMELL-BOUND"

150. **Jumbles:** SHEAF FOAMY INLAND OPENLY
Answer: What the egotistical nudist was all wrapped up in—ONLY HIMSELF

151. **Jumbles:** CHESS MIRTH SHREWD PITIED
Answer: What a miniskirt is—A "TEMPT-DRESS"

152. **Jumbles:** CLOUT BALMY SINGLE BUTTER
Answer: What you need to have in order to be an organ grinder—A TURN FOR MUSIC

153. **Jumbles:** COMET WEIGH YEOMAN TAUGHT
Answer: Why the cook hurried to the herb garden—HE HADN'T MUCH "THYME" (time)

154. **Jumbles:** SUEDE HANDY PALACE BEFORE
Answer: What the intelligence agent had when he stayed home from work—A "CODE" IN THE HEAD

155. **Jumbles:** BLOAT EMPTY PARISH IMPOSE
Answer: What the tree that everyone gathered under was called—"POP'LAR" (popular)

156. **Jumbles:** HEAVY YOUTH TUSSLE DISOWN
Answer: His aptitude for platitude creates this in his audience—LASSITUDE

157. **Jumbles:** ARMOR NOTCH TALLOW MEDLEY
Answer: Women detest flattery, especially when it's directed toward this—OTHER WOMEN

158. **Jumbles:** HAZEL LIMBO ACTUAL RENDER
Answer: A fire sale is a place where bargain hunters might get this—"BURNED"

159. **Jumbles:** TONIC JOINT APIECE DISARM
Answer: Some people who think they're "operating" in the stock market are sometimes this—"OPERATED ON"

160. **Jumbles:** BYLAW ADAPT WEAKEN SUPERB
Answer: The pessimist had a happy look every time he had this to report—BAD NEWS

161. **Jumbles:** HAUNCH DOMINO MISLAY MURMUR BICEPS CANNED
Answer: Found at a ventriloquists' convention—A BUNCH OF DUMMIES

162. **Jumbles:** INNATE PLACID VANITY GYPSUM MOSQUE SPLICE
Answer: What the boxer got when his wife decided to file for divorce—A "SPLIT" DECISION

163. **Jumbles:** RATIFY PURVEY POLLEN BEFORE ISLAND DENOTE
Answer: What swimmers do to win a relay race—"POOL" THEIR EFFORTS

164. **Jumbles:** AMOEBA CLOVEN UNFAIR LEDGER JAGUAR DINGHY
Answer: What the cell phone user called the highway toll—A ROAMING CHARGE

165. **Jumbles:** BANTER QUAINT INCOME POLICE MAKEUP VELLUM
Answer: What he needed to do when his line broke—"TACKLE" THE PROBLEM

166. **Jumbles:** AVOWAL EMERGE EULOGY HELMET PIGPEN BARREN
Answer: The electrician gave this regarding his young apprentice—A "GLOWING" REPORT

167. **Jumbles:** VELVET CHISEL AGENCY ABUSED TANDEM MANIAC
Answer: Positive thinking can lead to this in a darkroom—"NEGATIVE" IDEAS

168. **Jumbles:** FABLED INDUCT DECENT FIXING IMPEDE GENTRY
Answer: A herder might fear this when taking his sheep to market—GETTING FLEECED

169. **Jumbles:** JIGGLE FROTHY VALUED OBJECT TROPHY SEXTON
Answer: What successful divers have—"DEEP" THOUGHTS

170. **Jumbles:** MODISH AERATE TRAGIC DABBLE MARTIN TARGET
Answer: Where do high-ranking officers shop?—AT THE "GENERAL" STORE

171. **Jumbles:** INDICT UNSEAT BAUBLE HOMING DEVICE TRUSTY
Answer: What the orchestra played when the new conductor arrived—MUSICAL CHAIRS

172. **Jumbles:** HAZING INBORN CANOPY STICKY VANDAL RABBIT
Answer: When he went hunting, the conductor wanted to get—ON THE RIGHT "TRACK"

173. **Jumbles:** GIGGLE FASTEN PLEDGE ANSWER BEHEAD EXCISE
Answer: What the union boss promised the janitors—"SWEEPING" CHANGE

174. **Jumbles:** BIKINI SPLEEN BEAUTY ORATOR POTENT INSIST
Answer: What the doctor found in his crowded waiting room—PATIENT PATIENTS

175. **Jumbles:** BAZAAR NETHER FEDORA VIOLIN CHROME GIMLET
Answer: What the manager considered the dependable southpaw—HIS "RIGHT HAND" MAN

176. **Jumbles:** MEMORY JOCKEY EXCITE ENOUGH JURIST BUZZER
Answer: What she considered her sculpture—A "TOUCHY" SUBJECT

177. **Jumbles:** PIRACY OUTLET FLABBY INJURE VICUNA SECOND
Answer: Rehearsing for a play is this for a doctor-turned-actor—THE USUAL "PRACTICE"

178. **Jumbles:** NOGGIN KENNEL FORGER WISDOM ADAGIO GUIDED
Answer: Important for a trucker to do when he thinks about the future—LOOK DOWN THE ROAD

179. **Jumbles:** BESIDE BETRAY HAGGLE ATOMIC FUNGUS REALTY
Answer: A jumper will do this to become an Olympic star—GO TO GREAT LENGTHS

180. **Jumbles:** GROTTO UNLESS NUDISM CURFEW PODIUM UPLIFT
Answer: What the dieting Briton did at the racetrack—LOST A FEW POUNDS

Need More Jumbles®?

Order any of these books through your bookseller or call Triumph Books toll-free at 800-335-5323.